CW01498417

Prologue

I was born in the Spring of 1936 at a Nursing Home on Lavender Hill, Clapham, so named because in the 18th century, huge fields of lavender were grown in this area for perfume and medicinal properties. The war years of 1939–45 were therefore a part of my formative years growing up.

Life as a child seemed pretty normal–it was all that I knew–in reality of course it was anything but normal, not just for our country but most of the world. It was a hugely significant period in our history.

I lived with my parents in a semi-detached house in a cul-de-sac of only fifty dwellings about two miles distant from the Great West Road. Several large factories were built along this road and became a major target for enemy bombing, earning the nickname 'Flybomb Alley' in 1944 with the advent of the Doodlebugs.

During the war, London was the target for German bomber planes and both my parents were members of the Air Raid Precaution team, known as the ARP. This meant that I spent a large part of my early life with one parent while the other would be on duty–often in the evening checking on everyone's safety. Most importantly, ensuring all blackout curtains were drawn tightly so that lights could not alert German pilots to areas of habitation.

The sound of the air raid sirens advising the public to go to a place of safety and the sky being lit up at night by huge searchlights scanning the skies for German planes was a regular part of our life and I felt it to be strangely comforting. It almost felt as if everything that could be done was being done to protect us and keep us safe.

At the end of our cul-de-sac was the railway line. At night a huge gun would travel up and down the line firing at random into the open sky–an attempt to deter the enemy planes. When German planes were detected, the siren was sounded and we would take cover. I would go to my little place under the stairs and my parents had a place in the living room made of huge planks of wood, some were four inches thick, placed at an angle against a wall to give a slope for any rubble that may fall.

Dad had to learn how to ride a bike when he joined the ARP. One night following a raid, all the telephone and electricity wires were down so he rode to the command post for instructions, his progress being noted by flashes as he rode over the still live wires. The bombing had been very bad, the casualties high and he found himself retrieving a solitary finger to take to the Ambulance. Normally on seeing the sight of blood Dad would faint. It must have been the burst of adrenaline that got him and many other rescuers through that night and many others to follow.

Whenever we left home, we had to take our oxygen masks with us, our defence in case of poisonous gases. This was even the case at school where periodically we

In memory of
Samantha Ann Porter

31/07/68 – 31/08/23

would all have to sit in a room with our masks on whilst they were tested to ensure there were no leakages.

Within a five minute walk from our house there was a small parade of shops which I remember clearly: Mr Bullimore, the Greengrocer; Mr Penfold, the Butcher; Edith, the hairdresser; Mr Stallybrass, the Cobbler and Mr Williams at the Post Office. There was also a chemist, haberdashery, newsagent and an off-licence. Sadly, I have forgotten their names. Everything we needed was close by which meant we could get things we needed in between air raids.

Food was rationed during the war and we all had our own ration book. These books contained tokens which had to be handed to the shopkeeper along with the money. Without these tokens, people were not allowed to buy any of the rationed goods i.e. meat, sugar, butter, cooking oil, canned goods and even petrol and clothing. The brown books were issued for adults and blue books for children. Each family was told which Butcher, Greengrocer and Grocer they had to register with.

The shopkeepers also had their own form of rationing. If we were lucky enough to get a Chicken for Christmas–that was a real luxury–Mr Penfold would keep a detailed record of this and maybe if there were not enough for us one year he would see to it the next Christmas there was, we just had to wait until our turn came round again. Like Mr Penfold, Mr Bullimore also kept a log and families just went up and down the list waiting their turn for precious non-rationed food.

Sometimes there would be damaged fruit that could not be sold and Mr Bullimore would cut out the damaged parts and let the local children come and eat the bits that remained. Another treat worth waiting for.

I remember our pet rabbit, Swatty. Due to every piece of land being used to grow food, we could not afford to feed him, so very sadly my father took him to the butchers to be put down. The butcher was then horrified when Dad said he would be 'burying Swatty not eating him'. Not even in those days of scarcity would we eat our pet, so Swatty was buried in the garden and I was allowed to sprinkle a packet of pansy seeds on the soil. The following year the most beautiful crop of pansies bloomed and so I entered some in the local show and won! ... Good old Swatty.

At home we had our own system too with the rationed food; I disliked cheese and my father loved it, so I would exchange my cheese for his sweet ration: it was an arrangement that worked very well for the two of us, that was until Mum needed some extra sugar to make jam with. We would go to a local farm, Perry Oaks for fresh produce, especially gooseberries when we could (this is now under a runway at Heathrow, gooseberries and all).

When the war started the Government had made plans for children and those who were blind or elderly to be evacuated to areas in the countryside which were deemed to be at less risk. I was duly sent off to some relatives who lived on the outskirts of Grimsby. There was nothing wrong with my new accommodation, but I was terribly homesick and determined that I would go back home to be with my parents. After a couple of weeks, my father came to visit me, to make sure I was ok. He came without Mum. I was prepared and already had my case packed. He succumbed to my pleas and took me back with him. The guard's van in which we travelled was full of soldiers. I sat on a pile of kitbags and because I was low down there was very little air, the soldiers used their rifle butts to smash tiny slits for windows so that I could breathe. On arriving in London, we were met by the wailing of a siren and then home to a very disapproving mother. Nothing more was said on the matter and I spent the rest of the war years at home.

There were lots of things for me to be excited about; Saturday mornings were the highlight of the week and we would go off to the Cinema, a ten-minute walk from home. There were always interesting films to see and at sixpence (two and a half pence) it was great entertainment and we loved it.

On Fridays, my father would walk to the local fish and chip shop and buy our supper. It would cost one shilling and three pence (approximately seven pence) and I really looked forward to this treat.

My parents were also very keen theatregoers and went as often as they could. Due to the ever-present dangers, children were never left with neighbours and so it was that I accompanied them on these trips. At the age of six, I had my first outing to the West End to see a musical called '*Rosemarie*'. I was enchanted and have since loved musicals. This was followed by a trip to see '*The Lisbon Story*'. In this production, one of the scenes included an air raid siren sounding the alarm, then a real one sounded outside causing much confusion. The play was paused, the safety curtain was lowered and we were given the option of going to the shelters or staying put, then up went the safety curtain and the play resumed: most people stayed regardless of the danger.

Many outings were with my father as my mother's health was not good. She suffered after an ectopic pregnancy followed by puerperal fever. Both Dad and

I always had this shadow with us that she might not survive.

Dad was a keen football supporter and liked to go to Hounslow (the local team) most Saturday afternoons; eventually, he became a referee himself. Dad would take me with him on many occasions. Sometimes if there were to be away matches it would mean a train journey or a coach (charabanc) if we could get the petrol.

After a match in Aylesbury, we went with the team to a restaurant (all restaurants were only able to charge five shillings, a maximum of 25 pence at the time). The place was full to overflowing and we were lucky to get a table, men in uniform were everywhere and we learnt they were to be posted the following day. Then to our amazement, Vera Lynn (now Dame Vera) had arrived to sing to the troops. She also came over to our Football team and I was introduced to her, something very exciting.

Dad was allowed two weeks off a year from his employment. These occasions were very much anticipated by me as it would mean going to spend time with my mother's family who mostly lived in the Bournemouth area and there were a lot of them. Between them, my Grandparents had seventeen children. Grandpa, a widower with eight children (all in foster care) and Grandma widowed with a small girl. They married and eight more children were born. Apart from wonderful holidays in Bournemouth we also visited other family members in Trowbridge, Westbury, Bath and Bristol. It was of course only aunties and cousins all the menfolk were away in the armed forces. I did enjoy being in the heart of such a large family, especially as I had no siblings to play with. Mum was the only one to move away to live in London when she married Dad as he worked there and also had a small flat that they could set up home in.

I did not know much about my father's family, a cousin in Windsor, aunties in Southfield and Luton and an aged uncle in Hackney. We rarely saw them.

Prisoner of War camps were built all over Britain and the soldiers and pilots captured were kept in these places until they could be repatriated when the war was over. We children were forbidden to go anywhere near them. In the countryside, POW's as they were called were deployed to work on the land. One year while visiting an aunt in Westbury my father got talking to a POW who was working on the farm, it turned out that he was a doctor–Dr Harold Rhylan. Dad got permission for him to join us for a meal at a local pub. Dr Rhylan told us about his life before he was conscripted and that he was only too happy to be captured as he had trained to save lives not to take them. My father and Dr Harold formed a friendship and kept in touch throughout the rest of the war years. Following his repatriation to East Germany his letters stopped and we never heard from him again, I have often wondered what became of him and his family.

Although I do have many happy memories from my childhood there were times when it was difficult. I would listen to the bombs at night whistling as they rained down on us. I would pray out loud, "Please God don't let it be us". This was an often-repeated mantra.

One night a bomb landed in the next road, very close, a direct hit which killed all the occupants. The noise was deafening and the damage extensive. The blast shattered every alternate window in our houses and it took all the tiles off the roofs: strangely we had a glass veranda which stayed intact, but an Aquarium in it was sliced through as if it were made of butter. The power of the explosion forced nails from their property into the wall of our house which were still there when my mother moved in 1989.

My school friend, Anne, her house was completely destroyed, fortunately they were in the communal shelter with us so survived. As a result, she had to leave our school and the family moved up north to stay with relatives.

My Godparents home was also bombed and they came to live with us for a short while whilst they were waiting to be re-housed. I loved to go to visit them and would play with a miniature tea set they owned, but all they found in the rubble of their home was one cup which they bought with them and gave it to me, I still have that cup, the design was of the two Princesses–Elizabeth and Margaret Rose.

When the war ended Winston Churchill, the Prime Minister at this time seemed to be everybody's hero and he made whistle-stop tours around the country as a public relations exercise and of course, with an election coming up he was eager to meet the people.

His daughter Sarah was an actress and one evening we had gone to see her in a production at the 'Q Theatre' at Strand-on-the-Green, near Chiswick. As the lights dimmed an elderly couple were shown to their seats three rows in front of us. During the intermission I realised it was Winston himself and his wife.

Afterwards, we all rushed outside to wait until the great man left the theatre, cheering and clapping as he got into his car. I then went backstage to hopefully get

Sarah Churchill's autograph and emerged not only with the actress's autograph but also with Mrs Churchills who was with her daughter. She asked me if I had got her husband's autograph, I had to admit I was too busy cheering him with the rest of the theatregoers.

On another trip to Earls Court, we went to see Johnny Weissmuller, the Olympic Swimmer and actor, who rose to fame as Tarzan of the Apes. Dad suggested I go backstage to try and get an autograph; I did and my father was delighted. He loved collecting autographs and kept them all safe in books.

My first glimpse of the King and Queen in person was at the Royal Albert Hall, to say I was disappointed would be an understatement. I imagined they would be very glamorous and dressed in flowing robes and furs, maybe even a small coronet, in fact, I thought members of the audience looked more fetching.

When the end of the war was announced on 8 May 1945 I had recently had my ninth Birthday, what a wonderful birthday present. That day I had been to the Twickenham Lido with some friends and their mothers and I stayed much too late. I was sent to bed with bread and water; I was absolutely starving. My punishment did not last long. At 6.00 o'clock the longed-for news came over the radio and it was official. The excitement was palpable, already the road was being festooned with bunting–nobody went to bed that night.

Street parties were arranged, the tables set out in a 'V' design for Victory. My father dressed in one of my mother's evening gowns as the Mayoress of Whitton with a rather fetching hat and a not so fetching bicycle chain round his neck from which hung a saucepan lid, his chain of Office.

Where the food came from, I have no idea, the tables were laden with blancmange, jelly, sandwiches and cakes–there was also ice cream. We children had all heard about ice cream but had never tasted it, the anticipation was huge. We were allowed a few teaspoons each and it was truly scrumptious and the highlight of the day and something I still love to this day.

In the turning circle at the end of our cul-de-sac a huge bonfire had been built with an effigy of Adolph Hitler sitting on the top. As soon as it was dark it was lit with much cheering and whistling from the crowd. Everyone was relaxed and excited that the war was over, life could go back to normal. Husbands, sons and brothers would be returning, although for many others sadly life would never be the same again. We were free at last to plan for a future and to re-build our country.

In retrospect, my love of animals began as soon as I was brought home from the Nursing Home and my father's elderly cat Smuts had to be introduced to me, then at a later date we had a ginger kitten we named Whisky. How we fed him during the war years I do not know, there was no propriety brands of cat food in those days, just scraps from the table I guess. Whisky stands out in my memory mainly because at the first wail of the siren he headed for the piano where a rent in the backing cloth gave him access to the workings. There he would stay until the all-clear sounded, another quirk was his nightcap of warm milk with a drop of whisky, this came about when the vet prescribed it when he was ill. After that, if there was no whisky in his milk he wouldn't drink it. I do remember our pet budgie Peter falling into a glass of whisky and being a bit wobbly after. When Whisky died he was succeeded by Phsycie, a name I rather liked. It was taken from a radio programme in which George Cole starred–I think it was called '*A Life of Bliss*' and then there were the odd strays that stayed for a while and then moved on to pastures new–worrying for us but we had no choice but to get used to it.

I had many other pets after the war–rabbits, guinea pigs, mice, gerbils and was caring for anything that Phsycie bought to me as a trophy, usually alive and uninjured. I remember a swift that had flown too near to the ground and was unable to get back up to fly because of its wing span. The other birds were really attacking it, as soon as I arrived on the scene, they made themselves scarce. I examined it for injuries, nothing bad, so I cuddled it to myself to warm it up for about 20 minutes, I then held it above my head where it flapped its wings two or three times and it flew off–my good turn for the day. These little rescues fuelled my inner being to help animals. Little did I know what and how many animals would enter my life.

Another occasion was when I was invited to join a school friend and his parents to go to the Boat Race in the Dutch Barge on which they lived. It was moored at Teddington, so we set off fairly early and chugged sedately up the Thames to Mortlake. The flotilla of small boats that followed the race went past us at the finish the wake of which caused the water to become very choppy, a pigeon got caught by these waves and would have drowned if I hadn't made a fuss. Very quickly a dinghy was lowered over the side and the pigeon was soon rescued from a watery grave. We wrapped it in some warm towels and when it was thoroughly dry released it, none the worse for its rather impromptu swim.

My father had hoped that I would follow in his footsteps: go to college and then train to become a chartered accountant. I was more interested in the sciences. My exam results for entry to the college were very poor and he called on my Headmaster in despair. Mr Regan the head told him of my interests and suggested that I should take that path instead, well what do you know my exam results much improved when I was allowed to do what I wanted. My first job was at the Wellcome Laboratories in Beckenham, Kent, then on to Guy's Hospital to study Histological Techniques, followed by a stint at The Royal Dental Hospital in Leicester Square. Here I was lucky enough to meet Charlie Chaplin, as our Professor I believe was this great entertainer's dental practitioner and he happened to visit the laboratories. Dad would have loved his autograph, it was just not the thing to ask for.

I then had an ice-skating accident which meant I had to leave my job and stay at home for some while until my walking improved enough for me to commute to London each day. A neighbour found me a job as a typist/filing clerk where he worked and better still, took me to work each day in his car, which to me was a luxury.

I never did go back to work in the laboratories. I had met Brian where we worked, we courted and we married. We rented a property at Strand-on-the-Green. It was only half an hour's drive to work and convenient for visiting both sets of parents in Whitton and Surbiton respectively.

One of the first things we did was to get a kitten, a Seal Point Siamese to be called Joka. I was not too keen on this particular breed, but I so wanted a cat I agreed. I had heard they were very vocal and not overly affectionate. The year before we had met fellow campers with their Siamese and the fact that it went everywhere with them, never strayed and travelled well had appealed to us both. The die was cast and a visit to a breeder was arranged. We did not choose the cat, he chose us. The vocals of the Siamese are soon brought to a minimum once you understand the language. As Joka had chosen us he was very loving indeed.

Six months later we were on holiday in Wales when we decided to climb Snowdon. The idea being that we would leave Joka in the car with food, water and a litter tray, however, he had very different ideas and made it clear he wanted to come as well. He followed us to the summit only allowing himself to be carried when the scree towards the top was painful for his little paws. Needless to say, he ended up being photographed by nearly everyone we met. We took the train for our descent to the village of Llanberis then slowly walked up along the road to where our car was parked at the Pen-Y-Gwryd Hotel. When we arrived back at our camping site and told how Joka had done the climb with us someone came over with a small dish of tinned salmon for him which he thoroughly enjoyed.

Our home on Strand-on-the-Green made our local stamping ground Gunnersbury Park where we would take Joka most weekends and each year we went back to our lovely valley in Wales.

Now a big move was on the cards, namely to Yeovil in Somerset where Brian had been offered a job. At a wage of £19.00 per week it was not considered worth the move, the firm upped their offer to £19.10/- (£19.50 in the days when 50p could make that much difference). We moved, we bought our first home and with the idea of having a family, made sure that it was in a safe environment, well away from fast moving traffic, it could not have been better, our home bordered onto woodland and it was in a small cul-de-sac of only four properties. The foundations were cut into the side of a steep hill, so views from our windows were magnificent. We could see Montacute Tower and beyond. On a really clear day we could see the Mendips and for this privilege we paid the sum £3,250.00.

Our son was born in 1965. We named him Alexander. Life went on as usual, with the camping in Wales the highlight of the year. Sadly, Joka was bitten by a rat, Leptospirosis set in and he died. It devastated us. We were on holiday at the time, so he is buried in our lovely valley, he was only six years old. Even to this day, all these years gone I get saddened by his death.

After a while and missing Joka terribly, we got in touch with our breeder and as luck would have it, she had a litter of five-week-old kittens for us to choose from. I was hooked on Siamese cats by now so a trip to see our parents was arranged and then to Putney to choose our kitten. A Seal Point immediately took our fancy, (he so resembled Joka) there was also a Lilac Point who was so very affectionate that by the time we returned to Yeovil we decided we had to have him as well. They were called Jinx and Jester. We did not drive back to Putney to pick them up when they were ready to leave their mum. The two kittens were put in a box securely and put on the train to Yeovil Junction under the guard's protection. Shortly after Jinx and Jester arrived our daughter Gina was born.

As the children got older, I always instilled into them that if they saw an animal unless squashed flat in the road always make sure that the animal is not injured or in shock. To make sure they were ok, or did they need help even if they were going to die at least hold them until they passed.

After the cats had settled then the rabbits and guinea pigs arrived. Slowly and surely a mix of domesticated and wildlife became the norm of the household.

We had installed two mini ponds in our garden and they soon became the homes for frogs and newts. The newts were safe, but the cats would often find a frog and toy with them outside. Frogs squeal so I was always at the ready to rescue them. This state of affairs was not to be allowed and I knew a ditch full of toads where we holidayed in North Wales. First day away and the two cats were introduced to the toad ditch. Shortly after, they returned frothing at the mouth, a lesson learnt, they never touched a frog again. Toads give off a secretion from the skin which is very unpleasant to the taste. Our little ponds turned out to be very useful later on.

Over the years more animals arrived, often being sent by the local vet Bill Pethrington. Birds, hedgehogs, rabbits, etc. Bill ended up helping and learning so much about the wildlife I took in. My interest and care for animals and their welfare has played such a very significant part of my life and it still does,

This story chronicles a particularly unusual period when we became 'the parents' of a baby Swan.

The story of Gale begins

8th – 30th June 1981

My son Alex has a passion for fishing. For his birthday we bought him a licence to fish at the local reservoir at Sutton Bingham in Yeovil. He belonged to the reservoirs Fly Fishing Association and all his free time was spent by the water. So long as he had completed his homework and had eaten his dinner he could go fishing for the evening. At weekends he took some sandwiches, a drink and was gone all day.

On this particular evening, he could not wait to get to the reservoir. We had had a weekend of howling gales and torrential rain. Everywhere was absolutely sodden. Although overcast and dull at least the rain had kept off.

Alex and his friend Dave were walking through the reeds when Dave noticed a bundle of fluff by the pathway, Alex bent to pick it up and just a flicker of an eyelid showed there was life. All thoughts of fishing vanished; with it tucked inside his jumper and leaving Dave with the tackle he raced home to me.

"Here, I've got something for you Mum."

I waited, expecting to be handed an otter, a baby fox, maybe a badger–nothing prepared me for this small fluffy bundle he held towards me.

"There, look," he continued, "A cygnet".

1

I took it into my arms, looked at my husband and said the first thing that came into my head, "Well this is different."

We can only surmise that when the pen (female swan) was leading her brood to the water this little one may have been the runt and was not able to keep up with the family as they were being led away from the nest.

I wrapped the poor little thing up in warm towels to dry it off. Then immediately rang the vet for advice and with the proviso that if it survived through the night–I was to take it down to the surgery first thing the following morning. I cuddled it to me for most of the evening. Only once did it open its eyes. I did not know at the time that it had imprinted on to me and I was its mum.

At bedtime, I slept with the cygnet wrapped in a towel in my arms and surprisingly I did sleep, many years of experience in this sort of thing has allowed me to rest yet still be aware of my patients every move. Very useful when my children were babies.

She did survive the night and so the fun began. The cygnet took some breadcrumb pap, (a mix of good quality wholemeal bread with chicks' crumbs, water and pond weed. Bread in the '80s was much better than it is now, hence why birds don't do well on it now.)

mostly by my opening her bill and smearing it inside using forceps to imitate a mother's beak, however, this did not work as it did with other birds.

At 9.15am I was down at the vets as arranged and she had a thorough check. A little malnourished and only weighing 11oz. maybe a couple of days old if that, otherwise nothing to worry about. I went home relieved but at 11.30am I was down at the vets yet again as she had started to bleed from the nostrils. This time I left her for observation and it was 5.30pm before I got the message that the bleeding had stopped and I could collect her. During that time, I had to decide on my course of action. First I had to notify the police that I had a protected species of bird in my care and the same to report to our local RSPCA Officer, who fortunately I knew well and, believe it or not, even The British Museum had to be informed. I next phoned Slimbridge for advice and was fortunate enough to be put through to Sir Peter Scott. He did offer to take the cygnet into their orphan pens as did Abbotsbury in Dorset however by now with the family all behind me I had decided that I was going to rear the cygnet myself. Having followed the correct procedures and knowing my Vet would be behind me for any medical assistance that might be needed.

I do not know what the Vet gave her to eat but she certainly came home to me chirpy and full of beans. It was hard to believe that less than 24-hours before I did not think she would live. Until now, most of the birds I had looked after were crows, jackdaws, ravens and the usual birds we all get in our gardens. Occasionally, a bird is thrown out of the nest for some reason I have yet to fathom, eyes tightly closed and totally bald for want of a better word. One night I was woken by one of the cats pawing my face. Waking I was given one of these completely bald new hatched birds, eyes tightly closed but breathing, not in shock, it did not realise the danger it could have been in. I nursed it for the rest of the night and next morning started to feed it and kept it in a bag under my clothing for warmth, I called it Habibi. Habibi fledged and had a very good appetite but never flew and lived for 18 months. I was shocked to find Hibibi dead but the vet's diagnosis was something like spina bifida in humans. Maybe the birds parents knew it was damaged right from the start.

Going back to the norm for our household, the cats would bring the birds all home as trophies, also mice, voles, moles and even a grass snake on one occasion, lay them at my feet and watch while I examined them for injuries and if none apparent I would release them after about an hour. I would then dish out the treats to the cats which seemed to encourage them to bring back creatures unharmed. If on the other hand, some nursing or rearing was needed, or veterinary care then so be it.

The first hurdle had been overcome–the cygnet had survived the night. She was fascinating but like all infants she slept most of the time. I tried feeding her with crumbs of bread soaked in diluted milk. That night she was put into a box with a hot water bottle and the fire on a very low setting. At 3.30am, I was filling a fresh hot water bottle and trying to feed her, not with much success. During the previous evening, Gale as we had named her (appropriate after the weekend we had endured) took three swims in the garden ponds but was still disinclined to eat. Brian recalled that waterfowl usually ate food off the water. The soaked breadcrumbs were put into a shallow dish and offered whereupon she

started to slurp it up with great alacrity and then jumped into the dish in her excitement. I remarked that she would need a good bath as she would smell of sour milk in no time and then the light dawned. So upstairs to the bathroom, bath filled to a depth of three to four inches. In went some pondweed and the next half hour was spent watching a very happy little cygnet swimming and preening with little squeaks of delight the whole while. This had to be brought to an end though as her fluffy down is not waterproof and she was sinking lower and lower into the water. A last shower and then wrapped in a warmed towel and carried downstairs, she had a final preen and joined our tortoise 'Delilah' to sleep in front of the fire.

At 10pm a feed from her bowl of bread pap (which she already has started to recognise) the hot water bottle and into her box. This time beside our bed for the night.

I was woken at 6.30am with small squeaks and rustlings from the box, someone was hungry, so breakfast was served in a washing up bowl consisting of small amounts of wholemeal bread, duckweed from the ponds and Ready Brek.

I have a wall mounted set of kitchen scales so Gale would sit in the pan while I checked her weight, it should be some time before she reaches five pounds and would then outgrow them. Meanwhile she is running around the room stopping every so often at the bowl which has been left by the piano. She reaches in to slurp up some floating bread or duckweed and then will nestle down in front of the fire for a rest. The fireplace is becoming her favourite place.

As can be expected there were strategically placed old terry towelling nappies in case she makes a mess. I usually had timed her correctly and put her out in the garden when necessary.

I put her into her box while I went shopping for some velvet ribbon to make her a collar and leash set—a nice smoked salmon colour I think—then some special chick food and to the library for lots of books on rearing waterfowl. The washing up bowl was empty by the time I got back and she is definitely putting on weight and growing.

I made up the little collar and lead for Gale who was not in the least perturbed as she went for a walk round the garden as happy as any pup out for its first walk. She jumped into both ponds, even though she does not seem to like them very much. It was just enough to soak her collar and then up the garden onto some long grass for a rest. Her new collar and lead rinsed and hung out to dry. A quick rub down for Gale and into the box with a fresh 'hottie' which she sprawls out on top of, rather than beside it as other birds and animals I have nursed will do. Another preen and then to sleep for a while.

By now with some reading under my belt I had already purchased some chick pellets from the local farm shop and made up a pap for her which she found more to her taste than breadcrumbs and with a full tummy she settled down for the night.

The next morning after a few minutes snuggle on the bed we put her straight into the bath where she had a good swim, she ate a small amount of duckweed and then we dried her in an old towel, after which Gale stayed by the fire and preened. I swear this preening gives her an appetite, for in no time at all she was looking for food again.

In the afternoon, I visited an antique fair in Sherborne where Gale was the centre of attention and boy did she know it. I used my daughter's old childhood dolls pram for her to sit in while I looked around the fair and she was no trouble at all. Gale loved the car journey. Cars held no fear for her. However, she would not stay in a box on the passenger seat but scrambled onto my lap and then onto my shoulder so that she could see through the window. This was not an aid to safe driving I might add. Fortunately, I had taken the back route to Sherborne so the lanes were empty and I could travel at a slow speed. Eventually I got her to stay on the floor, but it was not for long before she worked her way round, until she was squashed between my seat and the door. I could then give her the odd scratch while driving with one hand on the wheel. This activity was received with ecstatic squeaks of approval and she was happy right there.

At school I was never good at languages however I found the language of swan to be very easy to learn.

In three days, we recognised, "I'm a might peckish, where's my bowl?" "Ooooh!! This fire is lovely!" "Mum—where are you, I'm all alone and it's a big dangerous world out there." "Put me down I don't want to get out of the bath," and, "that's nice, do it again," or "that's nice–I'll have another mouthful".

It sounded almost the same, it really depends on where we are at the time. The similarities between a mother knowing the cries of her newborn baby, the cadences of the cry and my understanding of Gales squeaks and squeals astonished me.

We are now getting into a workable routine, so life is easier. In the excitement of the past few days, we had completely forgotten the fact that we were going on holiday on the 20th. Later that morning I phoned the destination at Weare Gifford to tell them about Gale and more to the point would they mind if she came too. We only had a few days to make further arrangements but thankfully they were so very interested in our new family member that they offered to find a good strong box ready for her.

She had her breakfast in the bath followed by being towel dried and then cuddled up to Brian and the two cats on the bed. She then had a full scale preen to fully sort out her fluff. She has also gained two ounces. in the past five days.

She seems to have developed new words. "Hello there," whenever anybody enters the room.

A local farmer friend has lent us a galvanised steel trough. This is out in the garden half covered by a gigantic fern. Pondweed is added and Gale loves the whole set up as she can now duck-dive flapping her feet so she can tread water and flaps her funny little wings, all of an inch long. One side of the trough is level with the raised lawn so she can climb out at will. She is always supervised as she must not sink below her own plimsoll line, she won't develop her waterproofing for some time and just sinks when she's too wet.

A visit to the market prompted an experimental purchase of watercress which as it happens was spot on. She adores it and my local greengrocer has offered to keep me supplied with all the bits and pieces that are unsaleable.

Being kept in the incubator box (not plugged in) was not ideal. We are so scared of treading on her as she is almost the same colour as the carpet. The cat's basket (they've grown out of it) was fetched down from the attic and she has taken up residence with alacrity, squeaking her approval as she preens and takes her rest, popping in and out at will when the fancy takes her.

To keep her contented when I wish to work out of her sight, I will give her a crust of brown bread and she is so busy trying to chew bits off that she doesn't immediately notice my absence. I therefore get between 10–15 minutes without being yelled for, rather like giving a child a rattle.

That evening was spent in the garden run with the six baby rabbits we have. We tried this last evening with great success as she liked the company and the rabbits found her equally comfortable to cuddle up to when they were not nibbling the grass. We supervise this of course. There is a small box in the run for the rabbits to hide in if they want, for Gale it is too small. One over friendly rabbit had its nose savaged by a dog when it stuck it through the bars in greeting, therefore I am not taking any risks and they can run to hide if necessary. The contented cheeps are evident most of the time. Then as it grew cooler the rabbits went in to huddle up in the box whereupon the, "I'm lonely" squeaks rent the air. I moved the run so that the rays of the setting sun caught it, out came the rabbits and contentment reigned supreme again. Incidentally it makes for a lovely picture seeing them all sharing a slice of whole meal bread.

Members of the local camera club came in the evening. They were in the habit of coming to photograph the badgers, of which we had quite a few visiting from the woods. The sett was only a few yards into the woods and when we put up a sturdy metal mesh fence an opening was cut so that the badgers could still use their run. Brian built a stile with a platform on top so that we could watch them in comfort as they ran beneath us to get to the food, we had put out for them. On one occasion, a stale chocolate cake was on offer. The first evening they ate all the chocolate icing and came back the next evening to polish off the cake. The new fence also stopped the cows coming in, as one morning the old fence had blown down and I found a cow looking through the window, two more in the garden and the rest of the herd looking interested. Help! The farmer came running and the mesh fence was erected on the following weekend.

Back to the camera club. It had not taken long for them to get wind of the newest pet we had as children carry news fast. Over the next few months, they came to watch Gales' progress with interest.

Tomorrow being Saturday a 6.30am start to the day is not popular. It seems that Gale likes to eat at night so apart from the hot water bottle I put a slice of brown bread in her box along with some chick pellet pap in the hopes that she might sleep longer with some snacks to sustain her. It is 12.15am before I finally get to go to bed and I normally prefer early nights.

Hooray it worked–the snack supply I mean. It's 7.30am before I needed to go to attend Gales' squeaks for attention. Gina had gone down at 6.30am just to check on her. What a sight met my eyes though. Every scrap of bread and pap had gone. To get the last dregs from the bowl she had rubbed her head and neck in it so she could then preen it off. There was dextrose in the pap solution. She was very sticky right to the very roots of her growing feathers. She looked like a parody of a Crested Grebe and my word the state of the incubator box and utility room defies description. Tonight, there must be a lot more snacks to get her through.

She was put straight into the garden trough to clean herself. She decided it was too cold and jumped out. I took her indoors and she sat in front of the fire to dry off and preen and under protests allowed me to try cleaning the glucose off her with a wet cloth. I made tea for Brian and myself then went back upstairs while we watched her preen at the foot of the bed. A little later I carried her downstairs where she still carried on preening for at least an hour before falling asleep in front of the fire while I got on with our breakfast.

It is now 9.30am and everyone is fed and doing their own thing. Gale is awake and busy slurping up her breakfast with the added dextrose and adexolin drops advised by the vet and I have the incubator box and the utility room to still clean up.

The rest of the day was fairly uneventful. Gale spent part of the time with the rabbits in the run on the lawn. Occasionally coming indoors when she called to. She makes for the kitchen whenever she feels peckish. She is a messy eater and leaves water all over the floor, but it is easily wiped up on the polyvinyl floor covering. She has also started to follow us rather than just sit tight and squeal. Her preening goes on for ever and never seems to stop for long. Then she either falls asleep or starts looking around for food. Jinx and Jester the cats are interested as they cannot understand why I am making such a fuss over a bit of fluff. They have sniffed her, had their noses pecked, so have decided it's best to keep

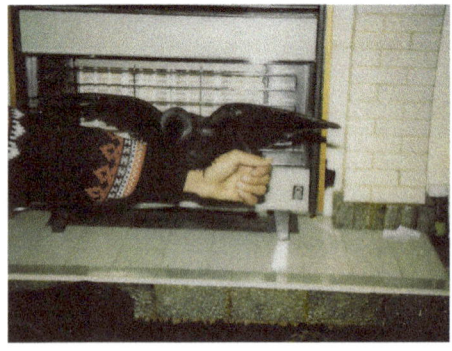

their distance. Kala (our pet Jackdaw who would not leave home) is not so interested at present–curious yes. She thinks that the best thing about this interloper is pinching from her food bowl, though I am not sure she likes the pap very much. As Kala gained more confidence, she started to fly pass Gale and try to peck at her tail at speed.

So far Gale has survived her first week with us. On waking this morning all was too quiet downstairs and we were getting worried. On checking her I was met by a very sleepy well-fed bird. The bowl of snacks was nearly empty, the greenery consisting of duckweed, lettuce and a punnet of mustard and cress have gone. Her fluffy down was a bit sticky, so I put her in the trough while I made the breakfast. I then dried her off, took her upstairs and while she preened I got some necessary swan reading done. By now Brian had gone back to sleep and after a while I'm feeling quite sleepy from all these late nights so putting Gale on a clean cloth, I dozed off with her beside me her little head against my arm —this peaceful state of affairs did not last long. My daughter woke us and a new bit of swan vocabulary was emitted, roughly translated–"Hey Mum, we've got burglars" followed with, "shouldn't you get a great big stick and investigate?!" Then as Gina entered our room, "oh! It's you–boooorring–Hello there".

The next day being a Sunday, we had some more camera club members coming over as the weather was really glorious, a perfect day for photography. At last Gale has got over her fears of the pond and we have to drag her out protesting loudly when she gets waterlogged.

It is a relief that she is happy in the run with the rabbits. At teatime we laid up the table on the patio where she joined us for a while to have a quick snack, then as soon as she had finished her meal she headed straight back across the garden to the run and sat down by the door waiting patiently for one of us to let her in.

She now weighs one pound exactly.

We are sleeping better now with no disturbances before 7.30am and with the snack bowl really filled to the top there is no activity trying to get the last dregs. Another bonus is that Gale and her box are not so dirty. She has put on a further one ounce and is getting stronger by the day. She climbs out of the cat basket with ease though very ungainly in her movements and tends to roll over the edge onto the floor regains her balance and makes for the food. Another option is if the bowl is close enough, she will just reach over with her lovely little neck and have breakfast in bed and the best reason of all for wanting to escape the confines of the cat basket is to be with her human family. Lots of creaking from the basket followed by a dull thud, flap-flap-flap as her webbed feet slap against the floor. This is not too popular from our point of view. Her calling cards can be large and messy though fortunately she is not inclined to explore too often and once by the fire and with us there with her she will settle down and stay put. I lift her up and place a cloth beneath her in case of accidents and we are all happy.

The days go past with the usual morning routine: she has gained weight again much to our delight, only another ounce but it is in the right direction. Most of today was spent in the aviary with the rabbits, although more sheltered, Gale does not like it and squeaked a great deal, she took ages to settle and then was only quiet for very short periods. In the early evening we drove out to the reservoir to see if her parents were about. Indeed, they were with the other five cygnets. How I wished that I could return her to her family hale and hearty as she now is, however, I did not dare to take the risk as it had been too long apart to try to reunite her.

I have never forgotten the state poor Kala was in last year when she flew off to join up with the other jackdaws. She just about made it home, crash landing onto the utility room floor, raw and bleeding especially under the wings. This all became infected and needed medication from the vet. It was a full two weeks before she ventured out again. In view of this I sure wasn't going to take on Gales' parents if they turned nasty towards her.

I had been brought a baby rabbit found abandoned (no doubt the mother had been killed by a car). Fortunately, we had Lucy a rabbit who had a young litter, so I put it in with these babies and Lucy didn't even notice there was a new addition. She didn't even seem to notice when I added Gale and they all just cuddled up to her with all the others. I am sure Lucy knew her family had increased but she so loved being a mum she fostered the baby anyway and apart from a demonstration as to who was the boss she did it no harm, just one big happy family. Lucy in fact helped nurse various birds over the years. When this little bunny was fully recovered, it was given its freedom, initially it staying close to home for quite a few weeks until it felt confident enough to go on its way, often popping back for a little extra food or just to let us know it were doing alright.

Gale seems to realise that I want her on special cloths when she is by the fire. The reason of course escapes her and after a feed from the bowls in the kitchen she will waddle back to the fire and settle down. Eight out of ten times all is well, then she will stop short with her tail end on the carpet. I gently push her the odd few inches. This evening as we were watching TV and I did not want to get up so in exasperation I ordered "get on your cloth Gale" and to my utter astonishment she lumbered to her feet and got on her cloth.

The latest addition to my understanding of swan is "Hey Mum, my food bowl is empty".

Her weight gain is encouraging, a full two pounds five ounces in the last 24 hours.

I spent the morning at the knitting machine out in the conservatory with Gale sat beside me, occasionally going off for a snack, however when I started to move with the intention of preparing lunch she started such a sustained and piteous wailing that I had to put her in the box. Giving me the chance to move quickly about my business and not have to worry about her getting under my feet.

Brian let her out when he came home and then after lunch, we inspected some plants that we had transplanted the evening before. Deciding they could do with some water I filled the watering can and Brian headed for the car, Gale was waddling around chirping her head off merrily when to my horror as I rounded the corner of the house, I saw that she was about to leap off the patio down into the garden ready to follow him. I must explain that we lived on the side of a 1 in 4 hill and the garden was terraced: as she leapt there was a thud which made me cringe, but it was soft earth sloping downwards. She rolled into the nearest clump of heather and was up on her feet unharmed and totally unperturbed by the fall. Anyway, we watered all the plants, cleared lunch away while Gale had yet another snack (where does she put it all?). Struggling with a bad bout of hay fever, I needed to go and lie down as my eyes were being forced closed and I was breathing with difficulty. I went up on the bed for an hour, Gale wrapped in a towel came with me and I dropped off to sleep, again lulled by her contented little trill type purrs in my ear.

Later that afternoon Kala came flying in and has decided that the light right by the television makes a nice perch. I think the warm weather and the strong breeze from an indoor fan playing really appealed to her. She will go out later and come when it is dusk. We just call her and she flies in through the bathroom window and has a perch over the bathtub with a metal tray for hygienic reasons.

With the holiday fast approaching and much to do, Gale had spent most of the day in the rabbit run.

The holiday is to be self-catering so Gina and I went out for some last-minute shopping. Brian had gone to sleep in the chair and Gale soon alerted him to the fact that we had returned by squealing her excitement. No other car has this effect so we think she must recognise the sound of our car engine.

As I did the ironing the usual programme was adhered to. Once again, she stopped short of the cloth, the order was given and she moved to the correct position immediately, that first time was not a fluke.

20 June 1981. Now for the fun, we are off to Weare Gifford in Devon for a week-long holiday. In the past we had always camped at Llyn Dynas, a farm in the Gwynant Valley at the foot of Snowdon, travelling overnight so that the children could sleep. This now is going to be very different, a self-catering holiday in a flat. For once we thought we would be animal free as

the cats and rabbits would be looked after by Joy our neighbour next door. Instead, we have a 13-day old cygnet. We had of course told them of our new family member and it could not have been better as in January they had had some interlinking ponds dug out in the fields quite close to the homestead.

The journey was uneventful and most enjoyable. Gale does like trips in the car especially as I was not doing the driving, she could sit on my lap in comfort, looking out of the window and commenting on all and everything. We had a large bowl of duckweed with us for Gales' lunch and when we stopped at an Inn for a rest and some refreshment she decided that a Ploughman's Lunch (less the cheese) was much more to her liking and even scorned the water bowl to try 'Lilt' and some lager to wash it down.

Our holiday venue was perfect, our hosts charming and the flat delightful and as for the ponds they were perfect for Gale. Gwen, Alan and John (we would meet their daughter later) were enchanted with Gale and after all greetings were made we took her to the smallest pond, she loved it, burying her bill in the mud, eating the algae that was floating on the surface, ducking her head in and out of the water and flapping her weeny little wings. Then suddenly exhaustion took over. I scooped her up and she was asleep before I had taken a couple of steps. Now at least we could unpack and check out the flat, get our supper and relax. Famous last words.

We must have arrived at Weare Gifford at about 4pm and all sorted by 7pm. Brian and the children were going out on a recce and I was going to relax in a nice hot bath. It was not long however before they were back. They had found an injured baby buzzard. I had no equipment, not even gloves. We wrapped the bird up very carefully and examined it closely but found nothing to cause alarm and with the help of our hosts who lent us a large cage we left it to recover while Brian phoned the bird specialist in Mortehoe, who was going to pick the buzzard up tomorrow. He could not give us a time so suggested we just went out as planned and he would pick up the bird whenever he could.

Our hosts have five large labradors and understandably they are very curious, not in the least aggressive. I introduced Gale to each of them. If they got too close, she just hissed or pecked their noses as she had done with our cats.

I cannot believe my luck that she has been quiet for so long. I gave her a meal of chick pellets at 6.00pm and after a short preen she fell asleep on the kitchen floor. The journey must have tired her out. I did place the carry cage over her as a precaution. The dogs are in and out all the time and I did not want them treading on her. Other than contented little trills I would never have known she was there. We have settled in nicely, unpacked and eaten our supper. I had washed Gale's nappies and now they are drying on the line in the evening sunshine. When she eventually woke up we took Gale out to the ponds again and for half an hour she explored all the little gullies that interlinked them and what looked like scum on the surface of one of the ponds was in fact floating grass seeds, she was ecstatic and gorged herself.

As the light was fading, we went back inside, all had hot drink and off to bed. We were all exhausted.

The next morning, we were woken at about 7.30am. As per usual I tended to Gales needs first followed by making a much-needed tea, (Alex and Gina were out for the count) and then we also dozed off again, Gale by my side with an arm around her to prevent any movement causing her to fall off the bed.

A late breakfast and out to the ponds. We had to fish Gale out with a long-handled landing net as she could not find a beaching place. The larger pond has a channel leading out of it and with a bit of coaxing she will swim along it until we can get to her.

We had a late lunch, settled Gale in her cage and went out for the afternoon. On our return we had the usual greeting, seemingly not in the least perturbed at being left alone.

That evening we invited our hosts to come up to the flat where Gale and the dogs were all sprawled out in front of the television set, incredible. This total acceptance on the dogs' part set another chain of events we were not expecting.

After another good night, our fluffy alarm clock not going off until well after 8.00am. On goes the kettle, Gale into the sink and generally the same routine we follow at home.

Our hosts had been toying with the idea of getting some ducks on the ponds for some time but were concerned in case the dogs chased them or even killed them. Now with some trepidation they made the decision to get the ducks and that evening their daughter went to collect some Muscovy ducks and a drake. They were transferred to an island in one of ponds, shut in for the night, well fed and the next morning a grand releasing ceremony was planned fingers-crossed they don't 'up jack' and fly away.

Once again, we went out to look around the area, leaving Gale for a little longer this time. No visible signs of distress on our return, yet leave her alone while we are in another room and she squeals loudly and most piteously.

The next morning, we stayed at home, Gale swam in the pond where we had left the ducks and they stayed away. The drake zoomed across to see if she was any threat to his harem and then left her entirely alone. She is growing at an alarming rate now and she can get out of the larger pond with ease. If we walk off, she will follow as fast as she can, even to the extent of coming across the bridge rather than swimming the stream.

We had at last found some duckweed at Jennets reservoir. We gave half of it to Gale and enjoyed her obvious relish at this missing delicacy from her diet. At supper time the remaining half was offered and then with horror we watched her gag on some nylon line. We pulled about three inches out of her beak and when no more was forthcoming, we cut it very close so as small a length as possible be left in her throat. The greatest worry was if the hook was in her as well. Everything pointed to this not being the case, but we planned to get her X-rayed in the morning.

After a restless night on our part, I phoned for an appointment at the vets in Bideford. By 9.45am Gale had been X-rayed. All our nerves were in tatters however she didn't know what all the fuss was about and did not really care. She had got a car trip out of it and seemed very content.

We were very worried so did not leave her and she came with us to Ilfracombe for the rest of the day. Later Alex took charge of her and she gave him no problems at all. We parked the car in a nice shady spot and went off to explore. We returned once in a while to check on her. Her natural instincts are very strong, once the cage is covered with a towel to hide her from prying eyes; no matter who returned to the car she makes no sound until the words, "Hello Gale" are spoken. whereupon she would whistle her greeting in return. The good news is the X-ray results were all fine.

Now knowing she is alright we took her for her first swim in the sea. All went well until she tried to walk out and was frightened by the wavelets in the shallows. In deeper waters she was much happier. I waded beside her and when I dipped down to swim she panicked when all she could see was my head. I quickly stood up again. I tried to swim with the same result of her panicking, so I continued to just wade through the water and all was well. Eventually we went ashore, me carrying her through the shallows where we were met by an extremely irate gentleman who let off a tirade about my cruelty to this bird and I was to wait until the bird specialist from Mortehoe who he had sent for arrived and my details would be taken etc., etc. I did not interrupt him. Then when he had finished, I took the liberty of politely informing him that I had reared this bird from two days old and that I was the wildlife specialist from Yeovil. I did not see the man from Mortehoe so guess it was all bluff. Come to think of it I don't remember seeing the irate man again either.

When the beaches had cleared in the evening, we took her off to find some rock pools. They were beautiful, deep and crystal clear. She swam, duck dived, splashed about and pulled weed from crevices in the rocks.

After this we went for a walk but unfortunately of a very short duration, we had to give up as the seagulls nesting on the cliffs were most interested in our baby and kept dive bombing us as they wanted a closer look to make sure we had not stolen one of their youngsters.

We picnicked by the ponds where Gale has learnt to swim for some time under water then pop up again much to the surprise of the Muscovy drake who chases her away from his lady friends.

I had bought my free-standing kitchen scales with me and Gale now weighs nearly three pounds, fully grown she will be about 20 pounds so quite a long way to go.

After an early lunch we went to Tamar Lakes to drop Alex off fishing while we went off to visit Bude.

Gale was quite happy to be left in the car while we looked around and frequent visits with offers of cress were gratefully received, by early evening we had left Brian with Alex at Tamar Lakes to fish the evening rise, Gina and I took Gale off to the coast again to a bay aptly named Duckpool.

Her slight trepidation at rock pools had vanished; Oh, what a game she led us–in and out of every pool we passed and in a very large one, she steadfastly settled in mid-pool well out of our depth and reach and put down her anchor. We let her be while we picked winkles and never a sound when we went out of sight. We worked it out that she must actually see us leaving her to get her out of the pool. This ploy worked miraculously. Seeing us walking away over the sands brought forth squeals of despair and she could not get out of the water fast enough. She came running after us as fast as she could, tiny winglets flapping, the squealing getting louder and louder, "please wait for me." "I don't want to be left alone," "I promise I won't go in that nasty water again," and so on.

Too soon our holiday was over and we were packing up to go home. A last long swim in the pools for Gale, a round of goodbyes and off to Yeovil the scenic way via Okehampton, Lydford, Tavistock and Princetown. At Lydford we stopped as I wanted my family to see the gorge. We decided to take Gale. So, after a good feed we took off on the three or more mile walk carrying Gale resplendent in her velvet collar and leash. For a while all was well and then showing such obvious boredom at being carried, she demanded quite loudly and with deliberation that she be allowed to walk. Oh boy!!! did she walk and loving every moment. She took us by surprise as on her leash she set off at a spanking pace and we certainly did not have to dawdle on her behalf.

At the end of the gorge is 'The White Lady' waterfall dropping some 100 feet to the pool below.

Gale was so excited she could not wait and she was into the pool immediately, much to the delight of some teenagers who were there specifically to photograph bird life in the gorge.

Returning to the car I carried Gale part of the way. It was slippery and occasionally there was gravel and I did not want her to get sore feet. Most of the time she wanted to walk, she liked being admired by the people passing and some even joining us to hear more about her. Foreign visitors were intrigued to see a swan walking on a lead. We have certainly done a lot for the English reputation of being a 'Nation of Animal Lovers'. One young lady even picked her up to have her photo taken though we did put a nappy liner in a strategic position.

We continued onto Tavistock, through Princetown (where the infamous prison is situated) across Dartmoor and home. The holiday a success.

It was soon apparent that Gale remembers home. Straight to her place in front of the fire, then to the kitchen waiting patiently for her bowls to be filled. Kala pulled her tail in greeting and when she went in for another tug Gale had to move much faster in her ungainly manner to get out of the way of Kalas sharp beak. One of Kalas greatest joys was to tease the other animals. She would often chase the cats through the house trying to grab their tails or sit on Delilah's back as she walked through the house.

I had recently sown grass seed where the sandpit used to be which Gale tried to mow for me, nice, lush grass I had been nurturing now going down her neck fast, I was not overly impressed.

1st – 31st July 1981

This morning Gale weighed 3 pounds six ounces.

A shopping trip into Yeovil with Gale was very amusing. I had taken her with me as various friends were asking to see her. The first corner we turned brought us face to face with Lofty the local newspapers' photographer. He whisked us back to his car where he had left his camera, then off to the nearest zebra crossing for a picture of Gale going across the road on her lead. According to Lofty this was an ideal place as the zebra crossing was normally the quietest one in Yeovil, needless to say a lot of cars came. Many wanting to stop and watch what was going on, so we had some difficulty in not causing a traffic jam. Lofty managed to get his photos and sure enough in *The Gazette* that weekend was our picture.

Then we went on to Tesco's where I put Gale in the shopping trolley, on a towel of course and after an initial investigation of her surroundings she sat down and watched the world go by. I placed my purchases beside her, a lettuce was a not a good idea and she started eating it. The delight of the young children and the other shoppers fully recompensed the self-consciousness one feels when doing something different from the norm. Most of the staff were notified on the grapevine to come and see and I was requested to bring her again so that they could follow her progress. It may not be possible as her present growth rate makes me wonder how long I have got before I will be unable to cope with her away from home.

At 4.30pm I took the boys, Alex and Dave, to the reservoir for an evening's fishing. Gina and I took Gale to the water after obtaining the rangers permission. She absolutely loved splashing around but not going too far from us and keeping in the shallows.

I have decided to cut back on Gales rations. She eats a great deal followed by preening and then just settles down to sleep, unlike her family who swim around the reservoir always on the lookout for a tasty morsel–she already knows where the next meal is coming from so doesn't feel the need to move much.

Brian and I took her for a short walk through the woods a couple of nights ago and Gina with her friend Samantha took her on two separate trips last evening. It has been very warm and apart from two small snacks of duckweed Gale just slept in the sun enjoying the warmth on her back. She didn't fuss at all at the withdrawal of her feed bowls. We rinsed out her swim trough which she had missed and after refilling it we turned the hose on her–she absolutely loved it, we then showed her the refilled trough onto which I had floated some duckweed. Sitting down on the rocks above the trough elegantly stretching out her neck which is now seven inches long, she proceeded to slurp up the green delicacy, resembling a vacuum cleaner in action, the surface was soon cleared.

When close to me she is so gentle, nuzzling my face with her beak, I have no fears at holding her and looking into her eyes which are soft and gentle, not beady at all. She will breathe up my nostrils in greeting like horses often do. I have noticed she does this a great deal when she is relaxing, sheer contentment is still signalled by pretty squeaky little trills.

Supper time was a thrill for Gale, she was given her feed bowls back, one filled with her beloved chick crumbs (12oz) and the other with water. Both polished off quickly.

We have discovered that she has a penchant for ginger nut biscuits and also a working relationship with Kala. We had a wooden biscuit barrel that Kala could prise the lid off with her beak. We started putting the ginger nuts at the bottom and filling it up with digestives however Kala would throw out the biscuits she didn't like until she got to the ones she did like, leaving biscuits all over the floor. Then each bird would have a feast tucking in to the ones they did like.

Her vital statistics now are:

Gale now weighs three pounds 11 ounces.

Body – Tail to Sternum – 14 inches – Neck- nine inches.

Head – four and a half inches. Wings – four and a half inches.

I have always noticed that Gale's beak and feet were very hot, a digital thermometer disc placed on her webbed foot registered 104*–105* almost immediately, the thermometer goes no higher, so a definite figure eludes me.

Respiration: approximately 11 inhalations per minute (resting).

For the past ten days her fluff had felt slightly prickly. She is moulting and pulling at her down constantly, her tail feels like a pin cushion. Panting when hot: 93 inhalations per minute. Unable to get a pulse rate as yet.

Hey ho!!! Gale is in hot water again, or polluted water to be correct. We went to the Abbey Pond to raid it for duckweed. Gale decided to have a swim in the main pond which on her disturbing the water released the unmistakeable smell of petrol. Gina and I chased her for 40 minutes trying to get her out and to stop her slurping up the duckweed, she eventually tired of the game came meekly to the call of her name, climbed out onto a large rock where she shook herself vigorously and began to preen. I gave her about one minute and then approaching slowly I reached out and grabbed her by the neck said a prayer and swiftly dropped her on to the bank. Oh, she did smell!!! Home like the wind, Gina preventing a screeching temperamental bird from preening and straight into the bathtub with the shower full on and with some borrowed baby shampoo she was thoroughly soaped. It took several washes. Gale protested violently, slipping and sliding as she tried to run away, scrabbling and squeaking, trying to climb out of the tub and with all this activity she did pass a few motions so any polluted weed or water within her was expelled. I had noticed the greenery does go through her system very quickly, I think today it was jet propelled.

She was then rinsed very thoroughly under the shower. By now she had given up the battle to escape and was standing quietly. When she smelt decent, I squeezed the excess water from her, wrapped her in two warmed towels and patted her dry, she still needed another towel to get the job done properly. Now feeling I had got her clean she was allowed to preen to her hearts content in front of the fire, to her great satisfaction.

Her down is very thick and when completely saturated there is nothing of her, she looks like a chicken from the freezer with wet grey cotton wool plastered all over it.

Gale again seems to be losing weight slightly over these past three days, this may be the huge gain at the beginning of the month is being compensated for. She was very unhappy last evening after the shower/ shampoo treatment and she protested wildly this morning when I went to lift her making a very strange hooting wail, softly in her throat that I had never heard before, when she realised that no more such rough treatment was in store for her she settled down on my lap for forty winks before starting the interminable preening. I left her to it while I went to sort out the bedrooms. At 9.45am I put her outside and she had a breakfast of duckweed from her trough, thankfully her motions were normal and well-spaced. A short while later I offered her wet chick pellets and a large bowl of water, after consideration she stuck in with accustomed relish.

I rang Hatch Beachamp (RSPCA) to ask advice re-polluted water and treatment of waterfowl.

To clean birds, Co-op washing up liquid and not to use baby shampoo. Apparently, swans have a membrane which protects their eyes in the case of irritants. My reason for using baby shampoo thinking it would be gentle and safe was invalid. Fortunately, though no harm done.

The trip to Ilchester last evening was well worth it, the trough has a three-quarter inch thick layer of duckweed on it, Gale keeps returning as if she cannot believe her eyes and by 9.30pm she had had enough and wanted to go and lay down. She waited patiently by the aviary for me let her in, I offered four ounces of pellets for the night only half were gone in the morning. She was actually 'full up'.

By midday all the duckweed was gone. In the afternoon I scoured Nine Springs (a local beauty spot) trying to find a nearer source of supply and did find a type by the Hendford Hill stream. She didn't really relish it, so after school Gina and I went to Ilchester again this time armed with a large strainer nailed to the end of a long pole (a billiard cue in fact) we collected 11 pounds of the stuff. At supper time I weighed out eight ounces and within 15 minutes there was not a scrap left.

The day itself was somewhat hectic, an early visit to the vet to check on her progress, then off to visit friends. I rarely have my morning coffee at home these days, I just visit friends who want to see Gale and coffee is thrown in.

After this a shopping trip. Gale refused to be carried from the car, she wanted to walk along the pavement in her velvet collar and lead much to the amusement, interest and delight of fellow shoppers and their children. I once again lined the trolley with cloth and immediately she sat down ready to enjoy the ride. With hindsight I purchased her a lettuce to keep her occupied whilst I did the shopping. While in the queue at the checkout I stood talking to another customer, Gale seemed to find this very boring and proceeded to show her annoyance by ruffling her down, (I can't say feathers yet) and when that didn't get her noticed she tucked her head beneath her wing and went to sleep.

During the late evening when it became cooler, Brian and I set about the job of erecting the large paddling pool we had got from Tesco, though I do think Gina and Samantha had designs on it. The back yard patch has to be levelled, swept as clear of gravel as possible, a layer of heavy-duty polythene feeder bags laid down first followed by the fabric from our old paddling pool and then we can position the new pool. The hose wasn't long enough to reach for filling it that evening, a hunt round the garage and garden and I found a discarded three yards length behind the Wendy house so tomorrow I will buy a hose joining clip.

The press came today, a journalist and a photographer from Exeter. On the whole Gale behaved very well for the camera, until a photo of her in the car was required: she sat down on the passenger seat waiting for the 'off'– unfortunately no off–so she started an in depth preening session and we had great difficulty in getting her to look in the right direction at the right time. 'Patience is a Virtue' so they say, by gum the people from Exeter were extremely virtuous, another shot was wanted of her standing on the seat, we did eventually get it, my, what a job we had, she is a well-trained young lady and standing on the car seats is not permitted so she just kept sitting down.

That afternoon the paddling pool was duly filled. The duckweed was added and impatiently we waited for Brian to come home from work. With the neighbours looking on Gale was introduced to the pool, six feet long by four feet wide and 15 inches in depth. As usual her tummy came first and she started slurping up the duckweed, then as if she had only just taken stock of her surroundings, with trills of joy she started ducking over and over again, she also pushed her head below the surface and splashed her feet, it was a happy experience for all of us, such delight so obviously expressed certainly needed no words to be fully understood by us humans.

Downstairs at 7.30am, I made tea and Gale was released from her bedroom (the utility room). She walked through the conservatory and out into the garden where I put her into the pool and without

preamble she started on the duckweed, followed by a leisurely swim and much wagging of her tail. One very contented baby swan.

As we have not as yet worked out a method for her to leave the pool whenever she wishes, we are thinking a ramp or a large rock, Brian will be the brainwave here, after all he is an engineer. For now though we have to keep an eye on her and lift her out when she's had enough.

At 8.30am Gale had been in the pool for nearly an hour, the last 20 minutes ducking and swimming under water, wing flapping, preening etc. I sat beneath the veranda reading the paper and watching over her and she made it clear she was ready to get out, it is rather cool and I notice she is shivering. Once thoroughly dried off to warm her up she goes to sleep.

It was 11.00am, Gale was in the run with the rabbits, squeaking away which was unusual. I opened the door and she nearly killed herself in the rush to the pool impatiently waiting to be lifted in again.

A short time later *The Western Daily Press* having read Gales write up in the *Western Gazette* requested a visit to come see her. They wanted a story and to take photographs for themselves. At lunchtime Brian and I dined in the garden, basking in the sun accompanied by the slurping of a greedy bird. This duckweed collecting is becoming a bit of a chore, no matter how much we get it is never enough, two pounds into the pool at 4.00pm and by 8.00pm after two short swims all had been consumed.

She has grown out of the kitchen scales so I tried to use Alex's spring balance fish scales. It was not ideal and she was not keen to stay still.

EVENING POST, SATURDAY, JULY 11 1981—3

Fluffy pal

Mrs Pam Murray out on a shopping spree with the young swan Gale. Picture: Eddie Wood.

Pelican crossing? No, it's a swan. Four-week-old cygnet Gale crosses the road at the foot of Rackleford with her new mother, Mrs. Pamela Murray.

Gale, who used to live at Sutton Bingham reservoir is now at 55, Yew Tree Close, with its foster parents.

Mrs. Murray's son, 16-year-old Alex, found the cygnets, nearly dead, in the reeds in a storm (hence the name).

"It had been abandoned by its mother," said Mrs. Murray. "It had only just hatched. Now its completely recovered and follows us everywhere. It came to Devon on holiday with us," Gale loves travelling in the car and shopping . . . sharing the trolley with the groceries.

Mrs. Murray is not new to the role of animal doctor. Each year brings forth another allocation of ailing fauna.

"We've still got last year's jackdaw. We had three carrion crows one year. They got colds so we gave them cough mixture. Lots of rabbits, of course, a badger that had fits and a spastic rabbit. It couldn't walk so we made it a harness.

"I have not been trained as a vet. It's just sheer love of animals," she said.

Gale the cygnet is great shopper

By Tina Rowe

MRS PAM Murray can be accused of swanning around when she goes shopping in Yeovil, because she always has a fluffy grey cygnet in tow.

The cygnet, named Gale because it was found during a storm, lives with the family in Yew Tree Close, and is devoted to the Murrays.

She goes everywhere with them, and her favourite outing is a trip to the supermarket, where she perches on the shopping trolly.

The swan, now five weeks old, was found by Mrs Murray's son Alex, aged 16.

"She weighed only 11oz and could hardly lift her neck. I think she must have been the weakest of the brood and was abandoned," said Mrs Murray.

Now the youngster, found in rushes at the edge of Sutton Bingham reservoir, near Yeovil, is in fine form, and will be returned to the wild next spring."

The latest addition to her food intake is when she found the cats bowl with 'Go Kat' in it. That disappeared with great relish in no time at all. Another helpful discovery is that rabbit mix with molasses in it is most palatable, so we are now buying that in 25 kilo sacks. This will take some pressure off me trying to locate new sources of duckweed.

Gale is now growing at an alarming rate. At 10.15 am a cameraman from HTV's *Report West* took some photos of Gale for another article. As usual she behaved well for the camera, and we enjoyed the short sequence on TV that evening.

Later that afternoon I went off to Huntsworth to collect Alex and his friend Nobby, they had been fishing all day and it was my turn to bring them home. Gale sat in the passenger seat chatting away as usual. On the way home we would pass the Sedgemoor Pumping Station and after obtaining permission we were able to scoop up 11lbs of duckweed from the water (beautifully clean as is to be expected) it took all of five minutes, so I will definitely be visiting again. Gale had to stay in the car, however because she could see us through the window she created a great deal of noise, the driver's seat being the nearest she could get to me was taken over, the outcome being that a newly laundered seat cover needed re-laundering. The passenger seat which had her covers on was untouched. A lesson learnt.

I put all 11lbs of greenery into the pool. Gale could not believe her eyes, she dug in with great gusto and at last conceded defeat. I lifted her out and she sits on the grass to preen, dry off and rest, until she feels peckish again.

Today, I have discovered a clawed spike where the joint is on Gales developing wings, very prehistoric like her reptilian feet and legs, it will be interesting to see if two more appear. I found this quite exciting, her dinosaur ancestry showing.

After our TV appearance we were invited to visit with people who had a lake on their property quite local to us, only at East Coker. Gale could really enjoy herself trying to upend without success but kept trying. She was able to keep going for much longer with her head under water, flapping her little wings and treading water–the confines of the paddling pool does have its drawbacks.

We needed to clean out the paddling pool today. This is a long job as the water is siphoned out straight into the drain, it was well into the afternoon before the final drops of water could be removed with old towels and the sides rubbed down.

I put Gale in as the hose did its work, somewhat surprised when she could not float on half an inch of water she tried to stand up and did the splits on the slippery floor looking quite perplexed. I had left some interesting bits on the pale blue floor of the pool for her to forage and she found water snails and tiny fish, small twigs were spat out in disgust. She must learn to do this foraging for herself when she returns to the wild. Slowly feathers are beginning to appear on her tail and beneath her wings, also one or two small ones on the wings themselves.

She showed signs of wanting to get out of the pond, I did the honours and lifted her out. She headed straight for the kitchen; I followed only to find her pinching the cats 'Go Kat'. The rest of the day was without incident and we went to bed at a reasonable hour.

The next day, a little shopping, then a photo session in 'Boots' the chemist, her backdrop being the disposable nappy display. I get through quite a lot of nappy liners with Gale and they kindly gave us a box of 100 for the advertising value that the photographs might provide, the photos were also to go in the 'Boots' newsletter. Three members of staff had pictures with her and one young lady actually posed nursing her, for Gale this was slightly worrying and she cried for me, her mum. Her obvious affection which still surprises even me elicited a demand for more snapshots of 'Mother and Baby'. They very kindly weighed her in the baby scales, a photo taken to join the many other newborn baby photos on the wall.

No weight gained. Her tail is beginning to sprout feathers which are dark grey also a line beneath each wing on her body is quite getting well developed.

My mother and father are on holiday in Minehead, so we had a day out to visit with them. Gale was extremely well-behaved, sleeping on the floor at Gina's feet for most of the trip. We met up at their guest house and after lunch at a nearby restaurant we went to Selworthy, such a pretty village about five miles from Minehead. We walked beside a small stream, Gale on her leash beside Sheena my parent's dog. A little show of jealousy when a small pool was only big enough for Sheena and she didn't want to share it with a swan. Further on the stream widened and deepened so both Sheena and Gale could wallow and swim at the same time.

Our next stop was to Malmsmead, another picturesque village and then on to Oare to see the

Church where Lorna Doone was married and ultimately to Doone Farm. Here there was a watersplash and lovely pools, Gale was absolutely delighted, so also were the holidaymakers, especially when she would not leave the water and I had to gingerly pick my way through the shallows to get beneath the bridge, throwing small stones to splash her and encourage her to come towards me. This ploy worked and the laughter it caused when this great, soggy, dripping, kicking bird was scooped up and tucked under my arm as I headed for dry land, her letting the world know in no uncertain terms, "I don't wanna go home, I wanna stay in the water, put me down," so on and so forth, just like a fractious child.

It had been a lovely day and it was very nice to see my parents. They live near Richmond in Surrey, so this was a treat for all of us.

In just five days Gale has put on a pound in weight.

Most days are routine now. Once again, the pool was cleaned and fresh water put in. Gina and Samantha enjoyed a paddle whilst it was clean; this did not go down well with Gale and we were not left in any doubt as to her displeasure at sharing her pool. She threw an almighty tantrum which was highly amusing. Not something you would expect of a swan.

A trip out to Muchelney and I collected 54lbs of duckweed from a lovely clear stream, about three feet deep. No leeches present, always a bonus. With so much we needed storage space, therefore it was divided:- 14lbs into pond No 2, 2lbs to the rockery pool, some 3lbs to the paddling pool for Gales supper and the rest divided between farmer Newmans trough and our dinghy filled with water an unusual store cupboard but it worked.

29th July-Today is a special day. It is my parents 48th Wedding Anniversary. It is also the day that Prince Charles marries Lady Diana Spencer. Everything had to be done early so that we could watched the much waited for Royal wedding.

Gale is fast becoming an eating machine and has reached the milestone of 10 pounds in weight. Once she had had her time in the pool and eaten and all duties were finished we all settled down to watch the wedding. Gale insisted she wanted to be on my lap. Gina laid down across the settee with her head resting on the back of Gale and we were all comfortable for such a beautiful wedding.

The next day we are off to Sturminster Newton to visit friends. Alex and Nobby stayed at the Mill for some fishing me re-joining them at 3.30pm as arranged. After ascertaining that Alex would dive in and swim if Gale got into trouble she was allowed into the river; this time a new experience for her, she had never had to cope with strong currents before however she took it all in her stride. By now we could understand her very well and she literally begged us to join her, this was not going to happen, so when we were ready to leave we had to hide which soon had her screeching and leaving the water to look for us.

The 14lbs of duckweed on No.2 pond is now all gone.

Apart from large amounts of the interminable duckweed, at suppertime she got through two bowls of chick mash, three slices of brown bread and some 'Go cat' all washed down with a nice cup of tea.

1st-31st August 1981

Today she only took a small amount of duckweed throughout the day. Gale is now on to rabbit mix with molasses big time, in human terms I guess she is weaning. At suppertime she demolished a very large bowl of white and brown bread with two pints of water.

At the chemist her weight was down, rather worrying but I had noticed flight feathers developing along the wing edges about one inch in length and wonder if it is causing discomfort making her lose her appetite. I rubbed my cheek quite hard along her neck which she enjoys then keeping her neck rigid she will press back. It was hot and I took her out to the reservoir to swim, she wouldn't even go out of her depth, she wants me in with her.

We brought the children's playpen down from the attic and put her food the other side of the bars. This worked amazingly well in stopping lots of mess. Gale just poked her head through the bars for the food and didn't throw it everywhere. This kept her sleeping quarters much cleaner and less work for me. It also meant we could use this on our next holiday again, keeping things cleaner just wished I'd thought of it sooner.

Today our plan was to drop Alex and his friends off at the wildlife park at Cricket St Thomas and Gina and I would go on to Hornsbury Mill where Gale could have a swim in the lovely lake there. This did not happen as suddenly the suspension on the car collapsed on one side, so we stayed put. We had tea on the lawn by the cafeteria and the waitress kindly brought some lettuce leaves for Gale, she was delighted with them and then tried the Dahlias for dessert–not overly impressed with them. As usual she received lots of attention with head and neck stroking, she absolutely revels in her role as 'star', a walk through the grounds on her collar and lead stopping for numerous photos to be taken and requests from parents for their children to be at the other end of the leash.

We got to the river at last, the water on such a hot day was irresistible and Gale raced down the bank which was very steeply sloped and fell over herself quite a few times, but in the end, she made it. I fully expected her to make for the black-necked swans, full grown and just a little smaller than her, but no–she stayed out of their way, likewise the flamingos. She ducked and splashed, fed and flapped, making sure that Gina and I were always in sight. The fun really started when we made to walk up to the top of the bank to sit in the sun and be more comfortable and on level ground. There was a terrific splashing and hissing behind us and turning round two of the black necked swans had decided to chase Gale. She squealed in fear and protested that she couldn't see where we were and in no time flat she was out of the water and heading up the bank. Grumbling in no uncertain manner about these strange creatures we expected her to be friendly with, to prove her point she flopped down on the grass beside us, laid her head along her back and allowed everybody that passed to make a

fuss of her–'now these humans knew how to treat a 'star' and 'oh yes, what angle would you like my head at, my right profile is most photogenic'. She has turned out to be such a diva I am surprised she did not stick her tongue out at the black necks. A short while later a peahen walked up for a closer look and without warning it had leaped into the air and landed on Gales back 'a la fighting cock mode'. The next 20 minutes were spent chasing away peacocks and the rest of the black necks who had all come up for a closer look. One young cob (male swan) was brave enough to let me stroke him. Eventually I picked Gale up and sat her by my side on the rug, this sorted the dynamics out and the birds drifted off, we all relaxed and Gale went fast asleep.

Alex and his friends had done their own thing, joining us later in the afternoon. Alex came strolling towards us minus a sleeve on his new shirt. Turns out that while stroking the trunk of an elephant he had had his shirt sleeve torn off and eaten–there's no accounting for taste. The elephant was ok, the shirt never recovered.

Notwithstanding the general vote was that a lovely day had been had by one and all. A mechanic came to sort out our suspension troubles while were in the Wildlife Park, so all's well that ends well.

Abbotsbury called to ask about Gale's progress and then gave us a tip that swans like grass cuttings. My lawn had been cut very recently so my neighbour Joy from next door promptly got her lawnmower out and soon handed me a carrier bag full of fresh cuttings. We floated these on the pool, Gale ate steadily for over an hour, as we had run out of duckweed. This was indeed a great discovery. Her weight is on the up again, she was checked by the vet, nothing to worry about and then she lost 11 ounces overnight.

This is the second time this loss of appetite and resulting weight loss has happened, this time coinciding with the appearance of vestigial feathers. Could it be that as I had suspected earlier in the month that her feathers coming through are uncomfortable for her and puts her off her food: rather like an infant when teething.

The last weigh in before we leave for Cornwall–she has gained 4 ounces, it is a good sign and we can go on holiday with no qualms. Panic over.

The traffic jam on the Exeter bypass was enlivened for others by seeing me sitting quite calmly with a swan on my lap. Gale loving the journey and chatting all the way.

On arrival we were shown to a large caravan which was to be our home for the next week and a small outhouse was put aside for Gale.

We could not wait to explore and went to Land's End the next day. Gale thoroughly disgraced herself by climbing all over the car when we left her and making a terrible mess. After the long drive yesterday, I guess all she wanted was to be let out to play. Her time came of course, finding a rock pool was all that was needed. The tourists had a wonderful time making a fuss of her and taking pictures, she loves to be stroked and tickled at the back of her neck. I just sat back with my family and let them get on with it.

A priority is to find a suitable swimming place for Gale that is not too far from where we are staying. A lovely stream below the drift reservoir suited our purpose and she was able to paddle about to her hearts content and then she got the 'sillies'–ducking, bobbing, flapping her wings (bathing I suppose) and then she dipped her head and half rolled over onto her back, wallowing almost, this rolling activity continued for some time, she was thoroughly wet through and extremely happy. During the afternoon we went out leaving her in her room, to make up for this she was allowed to join us in the caravan for the evening and Brian fed her on GoKat and malted milk biscuits, her latest food fad and like a dog she will dribble in anticipation.

Today we visited Cape Cornwall and tried once again to introduce Gale to sea bathing. At first, she showed no signs of fear coping with the swell, she hated the surf. It was a shame that she had her head under water when the first wavelet broke over her, she was not impressed and wasn't going to try that again. Gina buried her in the sand to keep her cool until just her wings, neck and head were showing where upon she went to sleep without a care in the world.

The outing for today was Sennen Cove. A very large rock pool gave us the pleasure of walking or paddling with Gale swimming along beside us, definitely no swimming in the sea, that wavelet yesterday had put her off the idea for good. The weather yesterday was so pleasant that we decided to go back to Sennen Cove. The large rock pool was our destination and we got settled in for the day. Gina and I went for some ice creams during the afternoon and of course one for Gale, she had discovered some time back that these were rather 'moreish'.

At the end of each wing there are now small quills about half an inch long, with a single strand of feather protruding from the occasional quill, her cape is fully feathered and her second digit feathers are nearly three inches in length. Next to the wing claw there is a lump developing where presumably was once another claw. The Pterodactyl had three such claws on each wing.

All too soon we are packing up ready for the journey home. Swimming stops were made at Lostwithiel and Postbridge. After a whole day with no swims Gale was extremely excited at our first stop, she got the sillies so much so that Gina and I had to enlist aid to get her out of the water when we were ready to continue our journey. At Lostwithiel, while ducking underwater she banged her head on the riverbed, jumped and shied to one side, looked at the offending spot from about six inches distance and then ran from the water at speed, putting herself as far as was possible from whatever she thought had hurt her. At Postbridge, with her head under the water a sparrow mistook her for a midstream boulder–I don't know who had the biggest shock.

She has put on weight and her vital statistics are now: body length. 27 inches and neck length 13 inches.

Gale loves to go out to the pool first thing in the morning as soon as she is let out, she is a creature of habit though and even though the small door which leads straight to the pool is the easiest and nearest she has to take her usual route via the conservatory.

Within minutes, I was alerted to a great splashing and gurgling sound which led me to believe the pool had burst–I was very much relieved to find it was Gale having the sillies–I had cleaned the pool yesterday and she does love the clear water. she was charging around, ducking and diving having so much fun. Cleaning the pool is almost becoming a full-time job in itself, what a good job our water was not metered.

That evening Brian plotted a graph showing her weight development over the first 62 days, it would seem she is possibly advanced by a fortnight due to no shortages of foodstuffs. While he was thus engaged Gale was on my lap, Gina and I stroking her, examining her wings and feather growth, generally fussing, yet she just slept through it all, even with Ginas head upon her back within the curve of her neck, so very contented.

Whilst Gina had her piano lesson Gale was quite content to sleep on the lawn while Joy and I drank our tea in the conservatory. It was most interesting to see the reaction of a visiting cat as it settled in the shade of the rose arch, its facial expression when Gale squeaked and stretched her wings was comical, sheer disbelief and then perhaps the thought 'my golly-gosh–they don't arf have big Sparrers round 'ere. The cat froze in horror–stock still–it had certainly never seen anything like this before, perhaps his milk had been spiked.

In the evening, another visit to Muchelney, solely to collect duckweed. On our arrival home Gale dug in with no hesitation and proceeded to try breaking her record for converting it into instant guano.

The highlight today was a swim in Dr Bests' Lake. She got so excited flapping her wings and diving which is always a cause for amusement, she is not in the least bit fazed by the two dogs being in the lake with her, just hisses if they get too close to warn them.

The temperature today is high, so off to Nine Springs for exercise and where we will be shaded by the trees. Another area she loves to explore. We picnicked while Gale swam, then walked the pathway while she was swimming alongside us chirping merrily, no problems in getting her out either, we just vanished from sight and then called her.

The last day of August and we actually got to Hornsbury Mill at last and make no mistake Gale enjoyed the car ride more than the swim in the pool. She chatted almost non-stop on both outward bound and home journeys. I had her on the floor at my feet and a couple of times she dozed off for a few moments. Coming home though she insisted upon sitting on my lap which caused a lot of neck craning from occupants of overtaking vehicles, the windows were open and the comments of ooohs and aahs were incessant. Gale of course loving the attention. She nearly lost her voice greeting everyone. Whoever named this species mute swans, had never met Gale who just loved to chat away.

At the Mill she enjoyed swimming alongside us as we walked the path round the lake, she got very excited ducking and diving and skitting about for a few moments, then left the water to sit preening by us as we had tea, another short swim again rocketing out when we walked off and called her to follow.

So, right now we have two Siamese cats that behave like dogs, a jackdaw who comes when called, a rabbit that will nurture any other animals that comes into the house for care and now a swan who will take and obey orders. How utterly amazing and very weird!

1st-30th September 1981

We have a new postman. Thinking to take a short cut, he entered our garden through the back gate only to be met with the sight of Gale swimming in her pool. To say he was surprised would have been an understatement. He legged it round to the front door pretty fast, delivered our mail, asked a few questions about our unusual pet and never ever used the back entrance again. What a coward.

I had to go to Odcombe, and as usual Gale came along for the ride. It was very hot, so the window was down, she actually likes to put her head out and feel the wind rushing past her, just like a dog. In the village as we slowed down, her non-stop chatter was loud as she gets quite vocal not wanting to be ignored. Both pedestrians and passengers in cars, all wanting to stop and watch her. On the return trip we popped into my hair salon. Susan my hairdresser had asked if I would drop in with Gale. We ruined the usual efficient calm of the salon when I walked in with her, resplendent in her velvet collar and lead. She caused quite a stir and everyone loved being able to see and stroke a very friendly swan up close. As we went back to the car, a Scottie dog out for a walk with its mistress looked utterly shocked: his thoughts must have been on the lines of 'oh dear, I definitely had too much of the hard stuff last night.'

I belong to the craft circuit, I make candles, I attend craft shows and on rare occasions I teach adult education classes. Earlier this year the *Blandford Book of Traditional Handicrafts* was published and I had been asked to write the chapter on candle-making. I also give talks on the Art and Craft of Candle-making to WI's and similar institutions: for this I dress in the fashion of the 1850's. It more or less coincided with the discovery of paraffin (in Scotland) from this came a form of wax and soon tallow was not so popular, (it did smell pretty awful). I started to make candles as I felt they were too expensive in the shops. It all started out just for fun and to make gifts for everyone. However, it grew to a little business. My claim to fame is that the Queen has some of my hand hammered candles and Prince Charles and Princess Dianna had some for their wedding.

Yesterday afternoon, I had my first candle talk of the season and in the knowledge that I could return from my venue via Muchelney I took all the duckweed collecting gear with me. Imagine if you will, me in my long semi-crinoline dress, mob cap, dainty little suede bootees hauling out great loads of green weed from the stream, straining off the excess water and filling buckets of the stuff: it might have been an eyeful for passing motorists, yet so very much appreciated by Gale. I swear the stuff is like a laxative to her, it seems to go straight through the system almost unchanged, yet she must get some good from it as Lemma the duckweed genus is the recognised food of Swans: at home I just run around behind her with watering can at the ready, it must be doing the lawn a power of good.

The pool has been cleaned, fresh water added and duckweed placed on top. Gale immediately got the sillies and went totally daft for about ten minutes by which time most of the duckweed was all over the garden thrown forth on the waves she had created in the pool. I let her be, I was certainly not going to try cleaning up the mess, she could have it later. However, it wasn't long before she was calling for food and of course I relented, how could I not with those tiny chirrups and pleading eyes, in went some more duckweed thinking she would now have a good meal, instead of which two slurps and she had the sillies all over again.

She is so happy with life.

The next few days were a simple routine for a change–Routine: I am not sure what that means anymore.

Gale has now been part of our family for three months.

At 2.15pm a visit to the chemist where she was weighed and registered a healthy 17lbs exactly. (Just think, I used to have Alex and Gina weighed here when they were babies.) I got in the queue with all the other mothers and waited my turn. I have nothing at home big enough for her and trying to get her into Alex's spring scales was a nightmare.

Afterwards, we had a short walk through town by St John's church and back to the car. She enjoyed the attention she was getting, she always does, yet I still get the feeling that a ride in the car is the highlight of her day.

We went to meet Gina from school, then home to the mini pools now full of chewed up weed and lily pads. At 6.30pm we chased her up into her own pool with its grass cuttings and I gave her four ounces of rabbit mix, which quickly sinks to the bottom and then she can enjoy foraging for it.

At bedtime another four ounces of rabbit mix and a large bowl of water for midnight feasts.

It is still very hot, so in the cool of the evening we drove out to the river Parrett at Stoke-sub-Hambden where clear running water, trees overhead with the sun shining through the leaves, it was indeed very pleasant, calming and soothing to the thoughts.

Firstly, Gale had a good feed among the weeds in the shallows, then onto the weir pool where she was able to dive and totally upend herself, or tried to anyway, followed by her flapping and racing around. She had a bath and an attempt at running in the water while flapping her wings: the urge to fly is so strong she instinctively tries. She has also realised that flapping her wings greatly increases her speed when trying to not be caught, or when I am running away from her.

I have been in touch with the Wessex Water Authority and have been given permission to take our canoe out onto the reservoir with the sole purpose of teaching Gale to fly. We had noticed her mother had started to teach the rest of the family, so I guess I must keep up. Alex helped me to load the canoe onto the trailer and the ranger suggested we leave it by the clubhouse. I plan to start lessons on Tuesday, all being well.

With the permission from the Water Authority granted, I could not wait to get on the water and see if it was possible to teach a swan to fly. Finally at the water's edge I clambered into the canoe and paddled out a few yards from the shore. Gale followed showing her delight to have me on the water with her, a new experience for the both of us. She became incredibly excited, going round me at such speed and thereby making more wavelets than the wind was already causing, at one stage I was quite worried that I might capsize. She did gradually calm down and I headed for deeper water. After a few moments Gale could not swim fast enough to catch up with me and when I called, she promptly started to run and flap her wings as a prelude, (although she doesn't know it) to take off and fly.

She managed to cover about three yards or so before closing her wings and flopping into the water. We practiced two more time before she made it clear she was too tired. I had anticipated a long spell out on the lake however it was only 35 minutes. I had to haul her into the canoe and head back to shore. I dried her off, lifted her into the car where upon she fell asleep almost immediately. We went back home for a much-needed feast and sleep by the fire.

My supply of duckweed is fast vanishing, so I had to make a quick visit to Longload.

Today we had the second flying lesson which was an abysmal failure. Gale showed absolutely no interest whatsoever in flying. I had to carry her to the water which is no mean feat I can assure you–she clambered up me rather than sit quietly in my arms and was madly flapping her wings all the while. Me all of five feet with a similar sized swan in my arms (her wingspan is now 7'6") must have looked pretty amusing to the ranger–I think he was waiting to see if she took off with me frantically hanging on to her legs. After all this effort on both our parts she was only interested in seeing what there was to eat from the lakebed and all we got was a tails-eye-view, after which she proceeded to have a bath, paddled to the bank and started to preen. I dragged myself out of the canoe and with some difficulty caught her, as I have mentioned she will now use her wings for extra speed when I am chasing her, Crafty!!!

I put her into the water but by the time I was back in the canoe she had swum round to the boat beach and was heading for the grassy sward in front of the clubhouse. I gave up–lesson over.

Gale came in for a while during the evening as it was pouring with rain and she made it very clear that she was bored with being alone in her bedroom (utility room). My father was visiting us this time, so she sat at his feet in front of the fire which nonplussed him a little until he got used to the idea, he did not really have much choice. On this occasion a strategically placed nappy was not used, she stood up to stretch, turned round and left a calling card on the tiled grate; just like a toddler, will always let you down in front of visitors. She then went on to the centre rug to have a wing flapping session, showing off obviously, she had never done this before and it wasn't funny either, the resultant draft created by her massive wing span sent papers flying across the room followed by a snowstorm of downy grey feather's, she was in her first moult and developing white and grey feathers to replace the down of infancy.

By this time my father was looking distinctly disapproving, although we did point out that this was an experience of a lifetime, a swan in the lounge, sitting quietly in front of the fire (sometimes) was up there with experiences.

This did not have the mollifying effect we had hoped for and the comment was passed, "your mother won't like this I can tell you". I think Gale must have sensed the frosty atmosphere as she enchanted us all by not only taking a biscuit that my father offered her, she also polished off a cup of tea as well. In a mad moment Alex had put his cup forward saying, "would you like a cup of tea with your biscuit Gale?" One slurp and she was addicted.

A new day and I had intended to start Gale's flying lessons, but the weather was still very cold and blustery so decided to wait another day or two.

Teaching birds to fly is not a new experience, I have done it for years. The usual procedure is to have the bird perched upon my finger, then raising my hand slowly I will bring it down then up again gradually increasing the speed, the bird starts to flutter its wings to keep its balance.

The next step is to make a soft-landing pad at the foot of the stairs and literally just throw the bird down, this time it will flutter its wings to break the fall and after a couple of days it is flying round the room. It will then go into the aviary for a week, then a small door is opened at the top and the bird can come and go at will. One day a blackbird after a tiring lesson was perched on the top of a dining chair trying to balance on one leg while putting its head under its wing, this was achieved with some difficulty when Kala sharing the perch and watching with interest bent forward and gently pecked with her beak to see where the leg had gone–poor little blackbird after all that effort it landed in an ungainly heap on the floor.

1st-31st October 1981

The third flying lesson. After much chasing Gale was enticed to enter the water and she swam off quite happily whilst I fetched the canoe. Some ten minutes had elapsed and to my delight as soon as I paddled out into the deeper water, she flapped and ran across to join me. That was it though: no more interest at all after that, just paddling around, ducking, bathing but definitely no flying.

I'm beginning to feel I am a failure as a mother swan.

Gina and I have not been out to the reservoir these last few days and when we did go the fishermen were out in such numbers, we had to be content with chasing Gale around the field against the wind which made her very unstable on her feet. She was struggling not to become airborne and did not like the wobbly feeling at all. Her wings are strengthening daily and even when standing still and exercising them she is finding it difficult to stay on terra firma. When she became tired, I carried her back to the car and we drove to the other end of the reservoir where her family were making up to the Sunday trippers who came with bread for the waterfowl.

Our little one was interested in seeing her own kind, presumably hearing her own language, the others unfortunately were all full of aggression. Four of the young were immediately herded back to the water by their mum. The fifth stayed long enough to tell Gale to 'get lost' and Dad looked ready to attack at any moment. I found this quite sad that she was unable to mix with her own family. A little girl came up to us with crumbs for Gale, stroked and made a fuss of her, which strengthened her opinion that humans were much nicer than those big bird things.

My mother came for a short visit. To our astonishment Gale remembered her from our visit to Minehead in July, so no introductions were needed. Gale was so pleased to see her. Making her excitement obvious. That evening she was allowed in for a while and showed off her very best behaviour–sitting in front of the fire and chatting non-stop. When I cuddled up to her, she immediately bent her head over my arm, tucked it beneath her wing and went to sleep making the noises in her throat that resembled a purr.

Gale has made no bones about the fact that evenings spent with us by the fire are a jolly good idea. She will even tap on the glass of the door with her bill to let us know that "she would like to come in please". Last evening I put her in her room and put the clothes horse barrier in position with the intention of breaking this growing habit in the bud–no joy–she stretched out as flat as possible, paddled herself forward on her stomach under the lower rung of the barrier, into the conservatory and then, tap-tap-tap on the glass until we let her in.

Another visit to the reservoir for a splash around and maybe an attempt at flying. She can now cover a fair distance running across the surface, however at the least suggestion of a wobble and she settles down very suddenly as if she's got airsickness.

Today we are to have a new carpet laid. The men arrived early morning. Gale was in the front pool and we were notified at once that there were aliens in our midst. I was amused to open the front door in time to hear the comment, "Well it sure ain't a goldfish".

The furniture was moved out and a great length of carpeting and underlay was manoeuvred into the house and one of the men stayed behind to do the job. Of course, Kala chose this day of all days to pay us a mid-morning visit, with no warning this great black jackdaw flew through the door into the empty room, did a victory roll over the shoulder of the carpet fitter, harangued him with some very bad language and then went to the kitchen to see if there was anything nice to eat. The poor fellow was already in a state of shock when what he had thought to be an ornament started to walk towards him: it was Delilah our tortoise. I am sure he was convinced he had entered a madhouse. Probably wasn't wrong on that count.

We were very satisfied with the carpet, though Gale was not impressed–she has been banished from the fireside, so evenings are spent listening to her impassioned pleas to join us. She is allowed into the conservatory then all she does is stand by the door looking through the glass and tapping almost non-stop to attract our attention.

We all bide our time waiting for Brian to give way on her pleas.

This afternoon we are to make a call to a couple in the village of Compton Dundon who also have a swan. I gather Sydney was adopted from a swan sanctuary along with a pen (female), both pinioned (wings clipped) so unable to fly, their injuries making it impossible for them to survive in the wild, unfortunately his mate had been killed three years previously by a marauding fox. They had seen me on the TV with Gale and wondered if I would give Sydney a home as they were to move to Bristol and wouldn't have the right place for him.

Of course, I said would with no hesitation.

Gina and I entered the front gate soon to be met by an enormous Cob (male) very annoyed at having his afternoon siesta disturbed. He advanced slowly wings slightly raised, I froze, making sure Gina was behind me and at a loss of what to do a small voice behind me said, "talk to him Mum", silly me, the idea had not even entered my mind. Nothing tried, nothing gained. I hoped to not show any fear (in fact I was petrified). I just stood my ground as he came up–he was so big–he was wing to my shoulder. Suddenly he greeted and did the strange breathing sound that I have learnt from Gale. I reciprocated which made him look distinctly taken aback and then on impulse I tried Gales strange throat purr on him (the one that means I'm happy and contented you are with me) my interpretation anyway. It certainly had an effect, Sydney looked surprised, then bobbed his neck first to one side of my shoulder (wing) then to the other for nearly a minute, (I call it submission) after that I was allowed to fuss and stroke him.

We all walked up to the front door together, which surprised the lady of the house. Apparently, Sydney had not let anybody come through the front garden for years, we who knew no better had trodden where 'angels fear not'. Arrangements were made for when Sydney would come and join us.

It has now been a long break from reservoir activities, as I have a very heavy programme of candle shows and speaking engagements. Poor Gale was left alone quite a lot, however, Joy from next door would go in at regular intervals with some cress or duckweed and speak to her until the children came home from school so she would not feel completely deserted.

The day of the first show is tomorrow. Brian has succumbed at last and had Gale in by the fire, his excuse was that a colleague had visited with his wife solely to see our swan. The next night I was out again and returning at midnight found Gale sprawled out in front of the fire squeaking contentedly with her head on Brians slipper: he said he did not have the heart to put her outside, so all is well again.

To at least give her some wing exercise I chased her along the road and she seems to enjoy this for some weird reason.

We do have to be so careful not to leave the gate open, but accidents will happen as she takes off up the road on her own always passing the time of day with our neighbours. Mind you nobody ever thinks to bring her back home they always send for me–strange how she seems to intimidate people and yet with me there they love to make a fuss of her. A swan's reputation for being dangerous sticks, though the only occasion I have found this to be true is if they are protecting their young. As teenagers my cousin George and I were canoeing along the Hampshire Avon. (a forbidden pleasure). We were as near as possible to the reed beds thus hoping to avoid detection by the water bailiff. The first sign of impending danger was hissing and then there was this enormous Cob advancing down the bank towards us, his wings already raised and ready for a fight. His nest was nearby and he was determined to keep his family safe. We did not wait to negotiate, we legged it, (or paddled it) as the case may be.

1st–30th November 1981

Last month, my mother only came for a couple of days, this time she is now going to come for a week and is bringing her sister, my Aunt Olive. For me sheer panic catching up with all the housework, which does get neglected somewhat.

Again, Gale remembered my mother and was very excited to see her again, she did not know my Auntie Olive, who cleverly totally ignored Gale and to Gale that could not be allowed. Gale was now most interested in this new person. Olive was just about to put a biscuit in her mouth when Gale snatched it unexpectedly (made Olive jump out of her skin) Olive then offered her a biscuit and now they became friends for life. They were very much taken with our 'Star' and needed no second invitation to come to the reservoir. Gale herself didn't seem to have suffered at all from her two weeks confined to barracks; she bathed, dipped and by now her wings were strong enough for her to race some good distances across the surface of the lake.

After this we drove to the clubhouse to see a cygnet of like age that the RSPCA Inspector brought over, the first friendly swan that Gale had met but after the obligatory mutual greetings, she headed back to her seat in the car as she was not in the mood for polite conversation.

We all went to Hornsbury Mill after a visit to the market for some eggs and into the chemist for her to be weighed. I put Gale into the weighing pan and she was a good 18 pounds15 ounces. This loss of weight was a worry as in September she weighed in at 19 pounds 4 ounces and in October 23 pounds 3 ounces and now only 18 pounds15 ounces, however she is burning up many more calories with her wing flapping and take off practice. A visit to the vet showed no signs of malaise so carry on regardless.

Thank heavens we had such a lovely long day at Hornsbury Mill yesterday as this morning I have laryngitis with complications, so my mother and aunt took over until I was able to leave my bed. Once they felt I was strong enough they left for Fordingbridge where my aunt lived.

Alex returned from college enquiring not only after my wellbeing but also as to the whereabouts of Gale, who had gone AWOL. I had not answered the door as it was pointless with no voice and a caller had left the gate open. I heard Alex shout, "alright!!" and then after a short while came up to me helpless with laughter, "Mum—there is a policeman downstairs, you'd better come."

A young officer stood in my lounge visibly shaken and his two-way voice controller chatting away on his chest. Apparently, with nobody about Gale had walked up the road and some strangers had reported her to the police.

Up came our friend in his Panda Car "Yes Sarge–I've found the swan, what shall I do?"

Voice box, "pick it up".

Aghast at this order he told me that it was with great relief that at that moment my son turned up and saved the day.

I explained as best I could and expressed surprise as Gale is registered with the local station. I think he went away with the intention of telling his colleagues what he thought about them not checking their records before sending him on a terrifying 'wild goose (swan) chase'. Poor chap, it put years on him. On reflection I wonder if his superiors were pulling his leg. The normal procedure would be to contact the local RSPCA and an Inspector would come armed with a long pole with a loop to go over the head and even then wary action is called for—maybe the Sarge did know that it would prove to be the famous tame swan of Yeovil.

I am up at last–a little weak and wobbly. I have a squeaky voice, but I am at least up and about. Gale kept tapping to come in, so I settled her in the porch but when exhaustion set in I took pity on her obvious pleasure at having some company and wrapped her in a towel and took her to bed with me for the afternoon. Oh joy! –oh delight!! –she chatted, whistled, heavy breathing and did her contented throat purr then with her head beneath her wing and my arm around her we slept with no disturbance until well gone 4.00 pm. When Alex and Gina returned from school, they found me asleep with Gale sleeping alongside me. Hence the title of this book.

Our first trip to the reservoir for nearly a fortnight and Gale needed no help to jump into the car. She was so happy for a car journey that she chatted non-stop for the three-mile trip and stood with such excitement as we turned in at the lodge entrance. We just opened the car door and she was off, wings flapping as she went down the grass slope, leaving the ground by some four inches and then over the bank which gave her a further eight to ten feet of downward flight before she landed on the water. For the first time she did not wobble when leaving solid ground and seemed not to mind the feel of weightlessness as she proceeded to make three or four very long runs across the water though not achieving lift-off.

Mind you there was not a breath of wind to help her at all. Better luck tomorrow.

A RED LETTER DAY.
GALE FLEW

It's the 15th today, we went out to the reservoir again. Gina and I chased her to the water hoping that she would get enough speed for flight, but Gale was not interested. She sedately entered the lake and swam off, then suddenly raced across the water for some 100 yards or more, swam back proudly with wings slightly raised, snorting and whistling her delight and then magic happened-she turned, headed into the wind again and started running, the splashing of her feet on the surface of the water became less and less and then she was up, four inches, six inches–higher and higher and then she levelled out at about eight feet with legs dangling beneath her–she then tucked them up but maybe she felt insecure as she promptly dangled them back down again and then glided to the water. Not a good landing but she flew, covering about thirty to forty feet and at height, her beautiful wings carrying her quite effortlessly. So incredibly exciting for all.

She decided that was enough for the day–she swam straight back to the bank, climbed out and headed for the car. She preened of course but no sooner had we got home than she settled in the grass on the first terrace and went to sleep.

"Exercise may be good for one but really was that supposed to happen? I've never seen you do it Mum, you might have warned me."

The next day off again to Sutton Bingham. Gale showing signs of excitement when we got there but not too enthusiastic repeating yesterday's performance of flying, or for that matter doing anything that required effort. We were disappointed. Three small runs across the water and that was it. I think the fading light worried her and she would not come to the bank. Darkness fell and I had to go for the rangers help. Fortunately, there were no anglers needing the boat that night, so all the lights were put on in the clubhouse and after a few calls she was on her way to us like a shot. To Gale the lighted window meant warmth, food, titbits and she couldn't wait to get there. The only problem was heading her to the car and not the open door of the clubhouse.

The people from the *Sunday Independent* came again to follow up on Gale's progress and we all headed out to Sutton Bingham. We left her in the car while I fetched the canoe, geared up and paddled out into the lake. The young lady journalist then went to release Gale while the photographer was pre-warned by me to prepare his camera for immediate use. These plans were needed as on the car door being opened and my calling her name, Gale leapt to the ground and flapping her wings immediately started racing towards the lake, leaving the ground and flying the last fifteen feet or so at about six feet altitude making a perfect landing on the water. The photographer was elated as he had the shot he wanted.

After this she ran across the lake several times, bathed, rolled over, performed like a 'Star' for the camera.

On his asking, "will she do that again?" (to which normally I would have replied in the negative) to prove me wrong she repeated the performance over and over as if to ensure he got every photo and angle that he wanted.

A very satisfactory morning all round and such a relief.

Kala has us all puzzled by her latest behaviour. She will fill her crop to literally overflowing then fly out of the window only for a very short while and returns crop empty, then repeats the process three or four times. It is written that jackdaws hoard things and I was wondering if this is what she is doing; hoarding food for a later date? It seems unlikely when she knows there is always a full bowl for her here in the conservatory and plenty more in the bathroom where she spends the night.

Today it is my turn to fetch the boys from Longload after a day's fishing. We now notice that Gale's beak is showing a slight tinting beneath the grey of infancy so will in time be the lovely orange that we associate with swans. Another successful experiment this week was to throw out the large box and to make her a nest on which to sleep. She took to it at once. A large plastic tray lined with newspaper and then a thick layer of hay, Gale waddled over, settled herself down and turned her back on us, this was so much warmer than newspaper and hay on the cold floor. When we came down the next morning she was still in bed, whereas before she would be standing by the door waiting to be let loose.

It is now becoming an almost daily habit to go to the reservoir. As she raced towards the lake, down the slope and leaving the ground to gain about a height of four feet the impetus was such that she kept on with the obvious intention of landing in the lake but as she cleared the bank an up-draught caught her and she shot upwards some 25 to 30 feet. A very strong wind was blowing and she set off across the lake, undercarriage up, a lovely wing motion, neck fully extended, 'this is it' I thought, 'she's off' and then it seemed she realised that I was not following, she banked round to come back looking for me. She looked down in total panic–"Oh my golly, what's Mum doing down there, HELP !!!"

Down came her legs, she did not fall like a stone but by gosh am I glad she landed on water. No graceful gliding using her feet as water skis. She just landed as fast as she could, 'SMACK'–I bet her feet stung, not a belly flop–more of a feet flop. She gave me quite a long discourse on what she had just been through and "why had I not warned her what to expect when a strong wind blows up a nice girls wings," etc. etc. Eventually she calmed down, practiced making half a dozen or so take offs and landings but never once gaining an altitude of more than two feet.

She stayed in the water for a while, but with one further amusing little incident. She has never been very clever at upending, (swans do this to find morsels of food on riverbeds, ponds, lakes, wherever) today, she did it perfectly, tail vertical but it kept on going over, until she had done a complete somersault. She didn't like that experience at all. I was treated to another

tirade, presumably along the lines of, "if I couldn't teach her to upend properly, could she please go to college and have specialist training?" after which she went and made eyes at Pete (the ranger) and ignored me entirely and would not come out of the water until Pete did the honours. She had never gone to him before and I think he was quite chuffed.

With Christmas just around the corner, I have been very busy candle-making and Gale was getting bored waiting for company so she decided to go looking for someone to talk to. A friend popped over to collect some candles she had ordered. I greeted her and after a preliminary chit-chat I asked, "how do you like my swan?".

"What Swan?" was the reply and I knew I was in trouble. I called Gale and a reply came immediately but oh from such a distance. I raced into the woods but no sightings though she was still answering my calls with enthusiasm, next over to my neighbour's patio thinking she might be in her garden, no such luck but I could see her way down the hill sat on some rickety mesh fencing looking with interest into a garden some four feet below. I ran to collect her but seeing me coming she

SWAN
SONG
FOR GALE
AND PAM

SATURDAY MORNING shoppers in Yeovil's Middle Street had got quite used to seeing a lady name Gale accompany Normalair-Garrett project engineer Brian Murray and his wife Pam. But when Gale occupied the front seat of the Murrays car, many a motorist couldn't believe his eyes.

Pam Murray, wife of NGL project engineer (rotating machinery) Brian Murray, taught her pet swan Gale to fly by chasing her across Sutton Bingham reservoir in a canoe! The Murrays looked after Gale until she reached her full weight of 19 pounds.

Because Gale is a 15 month old swan who 'loves riding in cars and going on shopping trips,' says Pamela. Brian's 16 year old son Alex found the cygnet abandoned in reeds when it was only two days old. The barely alive bird was brought back from Sutton Bingham reservoir but the family did not expect it to survive.

However, thanks to the care and attention lavished on Gale — so named because she was found in a

storm — the young swan perked up. Soon she weighed 12 pounds and went on family holidays to Devon and Cornwall.

Gale spent her first week at the Murray household in the bath, convinced that Pamela was her real mother, following her everywhere. By the time she weighed four pounds she'd progressed to the family paddling pool! Later she was joined by a homeless Cob and the two became firm friends.

Eventually though, much to the disappointment of Brian's 12 year old daughter Gina, the time came when Gale and Sidney the Cob had to find a permanent home. She took her last car ride — to an all mod cons private mill pond a few miles from the old home.

They get regular visits from the Murrays who are always welcomed by squawks of recognition followed by a contented purr as the swans receive their bread ration!

jumped down using her wings to soften the impact. A beautiful garden with an immaculate lawn met my eyes. I grabbed an overhanging branch to lower myself down with the owners watching with amusement but no anger, they knew we had Gale so were not surprised at this trespassing on their property. The neighbour very kindly put on his jacket and came to my aid. We rounded her up and hoisted her over the fence onto the pathway above, the problem then was how could I follow her. After a few unsuccessful tries, dignity and decorum thrown to the winds and this guy, much taller than myself–(who isn't)–reached me down a branch and as I gripped it he made a step of his hands and pushed me up and over to join Gale. There is certainly never a dull moment.

On Saturday, Brian, Gina and I drove out to the reservoir where Gale had a good bathing session, a few races across the water and a very half-hearted attempt at flying.

Both days it was necessary to encourage her out when we were ready to go home, the weather was cold, blustery and trying to rain so we were not inclined to hang around while she did her preening which can last for anything up to one and a half hours at times. We bundled her into the car and got home as fast as we could, she can do her preening in front of the fire.

1st–31st December 1981

The weather is pretty dismal. We went to the reservoir, however, even Gale does not show much interest, I feel she wants to get home to the fireside which suits all of us. The weather stayed grim for the next few days, even Kala would not leave the comfort of the warm living room, so we timed her comfort stops and put her out leaving the bathroom window open for her to return when she was ready.

It was now time to collect Sydney from Compton Dundon. I felt so very sorry for his adoptive parents as they said their goodbyes. It was emotional for them however they did know he was going to have a new partner. We were happy to give him a home with us and we hoped a friend for Gale.

Initially we divided the garden up to be on the safe side and not put Gale at any risk. To our relief it was love at first sight. Sydney would not let her out of his sight. After a while we let them together. He followed her around the garden; in and out of the pools, feeding from the same bowls and even the odd preening of each other. That night I put him on a bed of hay in the garage.

The next day we were to have Gale ringed, Sydney had already been ringed some nine years previously–the ringing has to be done by law. This is like a plastic bracelet on the leg. Her identification number is Z34948. She flapped her wings when I picked her up as not too sure of this stranger in the compound. As soon as I said, "friend" she calmed down and was quite still while Trevor Squires from Stalbridge attached the ring securely.

Gale and Sydney seem to be forming a mutual respect and establishing a pecking order. She was a bit jealous at first or feeling miffed that he was getting a lot of attention and on three occasions pecked out at him, he was getting slightly jittery and gaining his confidence he had a go at her in return. A little later he had just got out of the small pool and was standing at the edge preening when Gale made a lunge at him. He jerked back, overbalanced and fell backwards into the water, Gina and I hooted with laughter and even Gale stretched out her neck and made funny little trills as if she was joining in the laughter. Today it appears that both swans must have sorted out their differences as there are still no signs of animosity between them, though I noticed that Gale is a bit wary at feeding times. Sydney is showing a natural trait that he has first sittings at any food and although hungry she is timid at joining him. I decided to give them a bowl each to make sure she was getting enough. This made her much happier.

The temperature had dropped quite considerably and the two small ponds are now frozen solid. Gale just sits on the ice squeaking for me to break through the layers of ice. She was in one pond and Sydney in the other.

On the night of the 12th, I put them together for the first time in the utility room (the garage was too cold). I put a sun-lounger between them to form a barrier. I do not think Sydney would hurt her, but I am not taking any risks. I went down a couple of times in the night and all was very peaceful. I am so eager to see them make a happy pair.

Kala's behaviour has continued to be unusual. Normally she goes out first thing in the morning and rarely returns until we call her at dusk. However, she is now coming in frequently during the day. I thought it might be the cold weather and guessing she needs extra snacks to keep her warm. She is still flying off with a crop full of food.

Gale and Sydney are still getting on well together, though they keep each other in their place if they feel so inclined. I will still keep the barrier in the utility room in place. Sydney is purring his contentment and is much gentler towards me. In the garden they share the back pool or have a pool each at the front which they will spend hours preening.

I think the Season of Goodwill must be getting to Sydney. He is being very romantic, letting Gale have first pickings at the breakfast bowls, then followed by a neck dipping session followed by a swim in the pool where this neck entwining is continued. I also noticed the feathers at the top of his neck were fluffed up, whilst the lower part was slim. For three nights now they have shared sleeping quarters with no barrier and sharing the supper bowl quite equably: it is lovely to look out there and see both with heads beneath wings, although attempts for a photo will always fail as Sydney doesn't stir while Gale always looks up and greets me. I have noticed that I no longer have to herd Sydney into the utility room at nights: I just open the door, say, "come on, bedtime" and he is in like a rocket. This evening Gale wanted to stay out for a little longer, (perhaps she was looking for Father Christmas) She preened a little and then had a nap on the back steps whereupon Sydney got up and went out to join her.

We leave the utility room and conservatory doors open and all the lights on until we ourselves go to bed just in case a passing fox gets too interested–If one thought he had found a stray turkey he was sure in for a big surprise.

Today is Christmas Day and the bitterly cold weather of the last few days has not upset the swans at all, even snow has been taken in their stride, frozen ponds were another matter entirely though. I have broken the ice for them every day in fact one morning the ice formed as fast as I broke, it so no swimming for a few days, then thank goodness the temperature rose a few degrees. I emptied the pool, removed all the slabs of ice and refilled it. Not a pleasant job I can assure you. Even hot drinks not withstanding I do not think I stopped shivering for an hour, unlike Gale and Sydney who were in the pool like greased lightning, ducking, somersaulting, wing flapping, the garden and conservatory looked as if the monsoon season had hit us by the time the two birds had finished their ablutions.

The temperature is still rising so I took the opportunity to take Gale to the reservoir for a treat and some flying practice. She loved the bathing, splashing and running across the water flapping her wings, but still not showing much interest in getting herself airborne.

It's time to leave and frankly I did not fancy getting in the canoe to chase her out. She was standing about two feet offshore in the shallows preening, so instead I stood about 20 feet back and called, "Come on Gale... OUT!! Come on girl... OUT!!!" and to my utter astonishment she waded straight out of the water towards me, stopping half-way to continue her preening. I then walked down to the water's edge to get between her and the lake (just to be on the safe side) and proceeded to herd her back to the car. She was one very contented swan.

It is very cold and windy and I always get wet legs when in the canoe, not pleasant at this time of year and when attempting to get Gale from the shallows she would paddle into the deeper water as soon as I got within three feet of her. Gosh, she can be an awkward little thing when she wants. If she continues to obey the command "OUT" it will make life so much easier.

For the rest of the week, Gale and Sydney seemed quite content to stay at home. I took Gale out a couple of times to the reservoir, but this did not elicit the usual excitement, it was still extremely cold with a bitter wind blowing across the water therefore we cut short our stay and headed for home, the ride in the car was much more to her taste. Also, I feel she is getting very attached to Sydney and wanting to get back to him.

1st–31st January 1982

Gale and Sydney have often performed what the books describe as a pairing ritual, more so since Christmas Eve when for the first time Sydney let Gale have breakfast before him: today they both enacted a slightly different performance: wings up and chests together, then head dipping, bowing and walking round each other accompanied by honking and squeaking noises through their noses, followed by a very lengthy bathing session, mutual dipping, entwining necks over each other, Gale nibbling at Sydney's feet and both giving the impression of being more delighted with each other than usual. I went back to the books to find some answers, this may be the ritual indulged in when they have actually chosen each other as mates as opposed to just courting each other.

Brian and I with Gina went to Hornsbury Mill and John the owner kindly gave us the freedom of his property to choose an area where we could build a nesting platform for the birds, he was going to give them a permanent home as they would soon need somewhere bigger than our small garden. We plan to take them over on Saturday the 9th. Gale will be three days over seven months, in the wild her own mother would have left her to fend for herself five or six weeks back, now of course she will have Sydney for company.

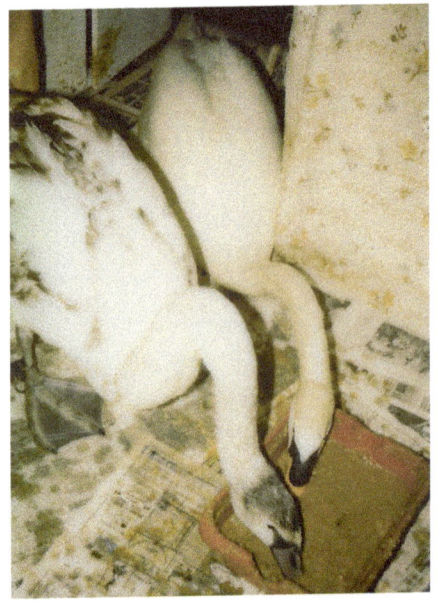

The best laid plans–ah well!!

A blizzard has set in and all plans for the weekend have had to be abandoned.

Again, Kala is behaving strangely, visiting several times during the day, filling her crop and flying off into the woods to return shortly afterwards, her crop empty. I started to have vague suspicions so on one of her trips I had my binoculars at the ready and followed her flight. Perching on the lower branches of a fir tree about 30 yards from our boundary were five other jackdaws. She was actually feeding her buddies and taking care of them. Mystery solved. How amazing and wonderful. She had friends.

On our last evening with Gale and Sydney we had them both indoors sitting by the fire and I was amused to note that Sydney showed signs of jealousy when I made a fuss of Gale–on impulse I picked him up and cuddled him for a while, honour satisfied I was then allowed to return to Gale and fuss her as much as I wished.

The thaw is almost complete so today amidst great hilarity Gale and Sydney were duly transported to Hornsbury Mill. My cousin Philip was visiting for the weekend so naturally joined the party, not without some trepidation. I assured him that Sydney who was wrapped in a large sheet would be upon my lap and Gale was a veteran where car journeys were concerned and would be perfectly happy travelling.

Famous last words!

I sat in the rear seat with Sydney wrapped up on my lap, Gina to my left and Gale to my right.

Before we had reached the end of the road (only four houses) Sydney was unceremoniously dumped onto the floor at my feet while I struggled with a very excitable wing flapping Gale who was most put out at Philip sat at the front, being in her seat (i.e. the passenger seat) and was determined to join him there. My poor cousin had to move pretty sharpish out of her way, Brian laughing helplessly as he jammed on the brakes and Gale squealing in protest as I dragged her back onto my lap. We now got her settled on Gina's lap, Sydney back on mine and off we went again. Sydney was marvellous, he sat on my lap for the whole trip, purring. Gale on the other hand was an absolute pest, she chattered continuously, she clambered all over Gina, myself and Sydney and dropped very wet, very dirty, very smelly packages all over us, thankfully we had been prepared and had disposable aprons on as a precaution, (we had wrongly thought that Sydney would be the troublemaker). When we reached our destination Gale nearly went berserk waiting for us to open the car door and let her get to the water. Having had no outings since Boxing Day she was full of energy and desperate to get out. Sydney on the other hand was so dignified in contrast. Once in the water together the two birds went through their usual neck inclining affection display and then just set about bathing, followed by foraging for food from the pool bed and both running across the water wings flapping, Sydney only doing this the once compared to Gales 3–4 times. I was delighted to see him even attempt it with his pinioned wings, I didn't realise he could or would.

We eventually left them at about 4 pm. It was a good job this visit was to be a permanent one for them, (or so we thought) as whenever we tried to get them near the bank for a final photograph, they both swam off, hey ho, we would be coming back.

I have always known from day one that Gale would have to move on, what better way than to a lovely setting of an Old Mill, privately owned and yet with the prospect of visitors especially during the summer months thus providing the human company that they both love so much. To put her out on her own would have given me a lot of heartache and worry, as luck would I have it I have been blessed with Sydney who also needed a home and they can therefore go as a pair. John and Yvonne who own the Mill will feed them and keep an eye out on their welfare, so all will be well.

Another unexpected blessing was the recent extremely cold spell coming as it did and postponing the swan's departure for nine days. If they had gone on the 8th Jan as planned we would have died a thousand deaths wondering how they were coping, as it was, they both loved the snow, giving me the only trouble I had ever had at getting them in at night. They slept outside on beds of snow all day and far into the evenings, never once going off for walks or seeming restless with their surroundings, the only irritation they displayed was the fact that they got very dirty being unable to bathe daily and they didn't like it. The ponds were frozen with a four-inch covering of ice again, the large pool had to be emptied, the cold was intense. Before Christmas when I broke the ice on the pools they would swim, however this time some instinct obviously told them not to, so after three days I stopped bothering. It was noticeable that where the neck feathers were wet from feeding (I floated the mix and bread onto one gallon of warmed water) little ice crystals had formed and they would shake their heads in irritation trying to rid themselves of them, just imagine if they had tried to bathe.

We were in touch with John and Yvonne to make sure all was well and for a few days it seemed we had made the right decision. We thought it would be best if we did not go to the Mill for at least a month so that they both could settle in and also that their new owners were happy with the arrangement.

Unfortunately, this was not to be. We had not taken into account the fact that Gale and Sydney were missing human company. It would seem that visitors to the Mill were greeted with such enthusiasm by two wing flapping racing swans that they quickly took refuge back into their cars and had to be rescued by whoever was free at the time. This state of affairs could not be allowed to continue, so inevitably, much to the delight of Gale and Sydney we had to collect them and bring them back to Yeovil.

Now for plan B.

The ranger at Montacute House suggested we tried Longleat, where the Safari Park is, for the swans to go to. We called and explained our predicament. This ranger was most interested and said 'to leave it to him'.

The phone rang one evening, Gina answered it, "Mum, it's for you, it's Lord Bath."

I was surprised, however he was very interested and wanted to know all the details. He then told me that he would be only too happy to give Gale and Sydney a home and a date was made there and then for us to go over to Wiltshire. A van was hired, Gale and Sydney loaded and off we go for their next adventure.

At first Lord Bath (this was Henry Frederick Thynne the Sixth Marquess of Bath) had thought the swans that were already at Longleat (of which there were many) might be a bit too much for my two to cope with so he took us to his private garden with a small lake fed by a stream. We released my two and without a backward look they swam off to explore their new surroundings. We made our escape as quietly as we could, so there would be no trying to follow us. It was heartbreaking and wonderful all at the same time. A new life for them.

Lord Bath then gave us the opportunity to look round the House or go to the Safari Park, we had done both on Gina's 12th Birthday treat, she naturally opted for the Safari Park. Something we both loved.

There is a notice at the entry to the park, "NO DOGS"–oh gosh, we had the two cats with us as we were also moving home. As it turned out we found that the cats were not at all fazed by the monkeys all over the car, giraffes and camels looking through the windows but when they saw a lioness approaching the

car they decided caution was the best policy, dived under the driver's seat and did not come out until we were well away.

I naturally phoned Lord Bath to thank him for our lovely treat and I did tell him about the cats: he was most amused. He really was a lovely gentleman. He kept me up to date with how Sydney and Gale were keeping.

One last story: Gale eventually flew over the wall of the private garden and discovered the beautiful ornamental water fountains at the front of Longleat House and was found bathing happily. Poor Sydney had been left alone unable to fly. This was not to his liking, so he promptly found a way out and walked all the way down this long drive until he found Gale and joined her in the fountain. They did try and put them back on the private ponds, however Gale flew out again promptly followed by Sydney walking the distance to join her again. This time Sydney and Gale were left and they eventually joined all the many other swans on the grounds.

We went to visit just once more not thinking we would never be able to find our Gale. However, after searching for a while we spotted Sydney and there sat besides him was Gale. She greeted me with her head up and little squeaks of recognition. She was now mainly white having lost all her baby grey feathers. Looking beautiful and elegant as swans do. It was just so wonderful to see her again. With Sydney and for her to recognise me my heart just leapt with joy. I only wish after all these years is that there may be her descendants still at Longleat.

I am eternally grateful for this extraordinary experience that I had.

Epilogue 2024

Now fast forward more than 40 years. That last summer with Gale was in fact the last Summer we were together as a family. As she was growing and becoming united with Sydney my own family were falling apart. As she was growing and finding strength, I too needed to find strength.

Brain my husband of 20 years was a Covert Narcissistic Chronic Alcoholic. He made life very difficult for all of us. With hindsight I now realise that it would have been better and healthier if I had left many years before. At the time though, I felt I was doing the right thing for my children.

At the end of February, I left Yeovil and went to my cousin Philip and his family in the New Forest. Our two Cats, Jinx and Jester, Rabbits, Lucy, Lady Slipper and Smudge, two guinea pigs, Ginger and Sandy and the tortoise Delilah all packed in a van came with us. Kala was adopted by my neighbours. Alex was already with Philip as he had a Unisex Hairdressing Salon and had offered to train Alex so that he had a skill. What Alex really wanted was to study fish farming. Gina was enrolled at the local school and I had to put my mind to finding somewhere for us to live, I needed to find a property to rent within my price range. Not an easy task as I had not two pennies to rub together. During this time, I helped in a craft shop and waited on tables at a restaurant to try and make ends meet and also continued with the candle making.

After five months I was no nearer to finding a property to rent and my father stepped in and bought a single unit mobile home for us at a local park and here we stayed for six years. Alex had long gone back to Yeovil deciding that hairdressing was not for him. He took lodgings with a friend's family for a while, then got a job and moved into his own bedsit. Understandably, he would miss all his friends and the area he had known all his life. I reckon he missed the fishing as well. Sadly, the family was broken to never fully recover.

My parents, Gina and I were now able to catch up on many missed years. For the first time my parents had a car at their disposal (Dad never learnt to drive feeling more at ease with trains and buses and mum had no sense whatsoever about steering anything which resulted in a few accidents riding a bike as a teenager), so we were able to spend a few holidays in the UK in more remote places. They did not have to stay near to bus routes and coach stations which was their usual practice. We would pick them up from Whitton and stay in pretty country villages and then return them to their home before we headed back to the New Forest.

I still looked after the odd wild creature and came unstuck with the hedgehogs of Hampshire. A weird rash developed on my arm and the doctor knowing my love for caring for wildlife jokingly asked if I went to bed with hedgehogs, I answered in the affirmative, the rash was Ringworm, it was six months before I was able to go rescue any more Hedgehogs.

Sadly, my father died in 1986. My mother stayed in Whitton for two more years and then moved to us in The New Forest. This was a good move for her as originally, she came from this area. Her brothers and sisters were nearly all within a twenty-five mile radius, she was the only one in her family that had moved to the London area and where Dad lived and worked. This meant she was able to reconnect with the sisters that still were alive.

She bought a bungalow in Barton On Sea. As we were about to become homeless, it was fortuitous timing and we moved in with her.

The arrangement worked well. I looked after the home, we shared shopping, cooking and laundry duties and mother looked after the garden (her passion), she was a very active Septuagenarian. I carried on making candles with all its ramifications and gradually had my own little wildlife sanctuary in the garden.

The local vets (only half a mile away) would send me the wild creatures brought into them for treatment, I never said no to anything needing TLC. I had kestrels, crows, herring gulls, black backed gulls, a woodpecker, a guillemot, pigeons, rabbits and a variety of garden birds, hedgehogs of course and even a neglected ferret who was utterly adorable. The kestrel stands out, as apart from having to be handled with extreme caution because of its vicious talons and beak, I had to buy from the pet shop a six- pack of frozen mice each week for its food, so against the grain, when I am forever rescuing mice that the cats bring home as trophies. I was so glad when I was able to release it. Over the years we had built an aviary in the garden and the garage became a rehabilitation ward–whoever heard of garages being used to put the family car in.

Strangely enough my cats always did kill rats even though they almost always brought other creatures back alive. I was once asked what I would do if I was brought a sick rat after Joka my first cat had died from a rat bite. This did happen and I nursed and cared for it as I would any other animal, it was so gentle and never once bit me as most of the others will do.

Over the years many little stories stick in my mind.

At one time we had a crow called Jasper who did not want to leave home–my mother and I would take the dogs for a walk (she had two miniature Yorkshire Terriers, Sophie and Lucy) the cats following and Jasper sat upon my shoulder. Jasper would love to sit on Gina's shoulder whilst she did her college work.

Jessie like all my cats was trained to bring his catches home alive. He would wake me up in the middle of the night to present me with a fledgling fallen from the nest, just tapped my face until I woke up. When flying lessons were out in the garden, should the young bird fly into the bushes out of my reach, Jessie would go in, catch the bird and bring it to me totally unharmed. Usually, birds caught by cats will let the world know of their plight, my flying lesson birds seemed to know that there was no danger to them at all.

A visit to London Trafalgar Square found me bringing an injured pigeon home from the square. It recovered well and was not in a hurry to leave, then a baby rabbit was brought in and I was running out of cages by now so I put them in together, very strange bedfellows yet I would often find them cuddled up together, one wing of the pigeon across the rabbit as if to protect it.

I do wish we had these digital cameras in those days.

The people of Hampshire use to be referred to as Hampshire Hogs, the reason being that hedgehogs abound.

The local vets would send me these wonderful little creatures after they had been medically examined and I would care for them until they were fit to go into the wild again and yes I still take them to bed with me, well wrapped up in a tea cosy as I will relate further.

Hedgehogs will take their babies out for a foraging trip at four weeks old and ten days after that will leave the youngsters to fend for themselves. If they are late births, i.e. late August to September onwards there is no time for the young to put on enough weight to get through the winter hibernation and many will die. They have to weigh at least a minimum of 600 grammes.

We had a very early fall of snow one year and a wee hoglet was found in a snowdrift, the mother must have been killed and this little one was near to death itself, it had not even been weaned. With warmth and TLC it just about hung on to life, after that for the next 10 days I bottle fed it every two hours both day and night, I now know why we have our babies while we are still young, hoglet was thriving, I was semi-conscious from no sleep.

When I would leave it the cries were heartbreaking, so I made a sling with a pouch into which I placed the hoglet, cuddled up to my back the cries stopped until feeding time and I was able to get on with my work, housework, candle making whatever needed to be done. To wean I trickled some drops from the bottle onto its tummy and he would lick it off, my daughter managed to get a short video of this. He grew and was given his freedom, however, for quite some time he preferred to stay in the garden and always came when called, he knew when he was on to a good thing.

Another hedgehog which came from the vets it was very poorly. I went to pick it up in the evening before they closed and apologetically they told me they had not even had the time to check it over, I took it home anyway only to discover on examination that it was having the life sucked out of it by 'ticks'. I wrapped it up warmly with a hot water bottle beside it while I thawed some goats milk, (I make cubes of goats milk ready for this sort of eventuality, hedgehogs get diarrhoea on cow's milk) and with a special high protein powder I get from the vets made a pap and fed some to the patient. I kept it warm overnight in the usual fashion, inside a tea cosy in my arms.

I now had to remove the 'ticks'. The large ones were easy enough, as they grew smaller and ever smaller it was difficult and it took me four days to eventually remove the last one and I counted in total 93 of the little parasites. The hedgehog made it and like some of the others did not want to leave home. It was rather satisfying to go into the garden at dusk, call Hedgy two or three times and out would come three or four of them to see what I was putting out for their supper.

On one occasion I had two herring gulls who continued to visit regularly for food. They would sit on the roof of my neighbours so they could see through the kitchen door and then call to let me know they were waiting for the food.

On 31 October 2004 my mother sadly died in her sleep shortly after breaking her leg. It was an end to an era and devastating to me. Being Halloween, it is an anniversary that is always marked. I do try to celebrate Halloween so as not to sink with sadness.

A year later Gina had moved to Wales and wanted me to visit for Christmas for the festivities. She didn't want me to be alone. I demurred as I had so many animals, however she would not take no for an answer and suggested I bring all the menageries. She is into animal welfare just as much as I am. At the time I was looking after my son's dog, so I hit the motorway with one dog, two cats, one tortoise, two painted quail and twelve hedgehogs. I remember saying a small prayer to the effect that, "please don't let me be stopped by the Police for any reason." I had all the cages loaded with the animals in the car and a small trailer to carry the foodstuffs, litter trays the Christmas parcels and my luggage.

Gina had a dog called Rowan, a Hungarian Vizsla who was very gentle and affectionate. I was teaching a sparrow how to fly, the door was pushed open just as it left my finger and Rowan came in, the bird hit him in the face and fell to the floor, my immediate thought was, "'oh dear, It's had it" but no Rowan had already laid down with the sparrow between his paws and was licking it very gently.

I went with a friend, Danielle, for long weekend to Amsterdam to see the bi-annual 'carpet of flowers' display at Grand Place. They have machines there to keep the streets clean and we were in Dam Square when I saw a baby pigeon (squab) had fallen from its nest and was about to be gobbled up by this mechanical monster, I just beat the machine to the bird and scooped it up out of danger. Next, I must buy something to carry it in, a souvenir stall furnished me with a shoulder bag, plastic lined, it was just the ticket, I still have it to this day. I guess this bird must be the only pigeon that has been to the Rembrandt Museum and the Anne Frank house. I had meant to release it that evening when we were at our hotel, it really was a baby and it couldn't fly, it was fully fledged and that was about the size of it. On liners from Harwich to Bergen I have fed pigeons as they sail across the North Sea, on cross channel ferries they are not averse to hitchhiking, my pigeon had to come back by coach. With my friend saying that if I was caught, she would deny all knowledge of knowing me and so we boarded the coach for the home journey. The squab never made a sound, at two comfort stops we tucked ourselves away in a corner and gave it some food and water. We did make it undetected and safely back to England. I put it into the aviary, no other occupants at the time thank goodness. I taught it to fly, just omitted to give it a map or the directions to Holland until it had done the six months quarantine required by law, in fact I held it for seven months wanting to be on the safe side. My daughter and son-in-law's comments on this escapade was, "if you were caught the authorities would think you were just a stupid old woman". Charming.

Now I am also living in Wales. A stroke in 2011 meant Gina driving through the night to get to Southampton Hospital to be with me. I was lucky in that I made a full recovery. Gina worked hard with me to aid my recovery. However, Gina was not happy that I should be so far away and in 2013 I moved to the pretty village where I now live not far from Gina.

I am still saving animals, I have four Siamese cats and one rescue feral all bringing me in trophies rabbits, mice, voles, moles, if one escapes into the house I just keep one of the cats in the room to find it for me and then let it go, also Gina often finds injured wildlife that she brings to me.

The acoustics in this valley are such that a dog barking some fields away sounds as if it is coming down the chimney, this concerned the cats at first, then Melody worked out that if she was locked out, she only had to climb onto the roof and Meow down the chimney, a lull in the television programme would let me hear her and hey bingo she was let in. Clever Cat!!!

The latest very surprising trophies are bats. I am woken frequently by the sound of a bats wings as it flies around the bedroom, perching for a breather on the lightshade while it ponders its predicament. There are doors that open directly into the garden, I open it wide enough and then wait for the bat to find its way out. Sometimes the little ones become exhausted and I can pick them up. I will warm them for a few minutes, then put them into a small hanging raffia nest I have in the garden–they will fly off when they feel up to it.

Now well into my eighties, I am still saving animals. I recently found a pheasant lying in the middle of the road, it was shocked and unable to walk, possibly down-drafted. I made it a nest by the radiator in the conservatory and had to force feed it for some days until it recovered enough to start feeding itself. I then started giving her some physiotherapy. I laid her onto her back wrapped up so that she could not struggle, then while in my arms I worked each leg moving it up and down gradually four times, then six, and then up to ten times four times a day. At the end of a fortnight this paid off and she took a few steps before collapsing onto the floor, another week and she was running around the conservatory, yet another week and Gina and I took her out into the fields, well away from the road and released her. She was so ready, gosh did she run, we were elated.

Some time ago, Gina had a runner duck called Quiver. He had a strange condition where he trembled sometimes uncontrollably and would fall over but he was such a character. He had been picked up by one of Ginas client's dogs and shook then dropped in a puddle, he was in the death throws when I arrived. I had noticed over the years that birds hold their necks at a weird angle when they are so ill and this cuts off the air supply, so for the next hour or so I held Quivers neck and kept him warm while Gina returned to work. Gina had put an infra-red lamp in place but was convinced he would not survive. However, after a while his body became calmer. His neck movements settled and eventually he opened his eyes. By the time Gina came back in he was sat up chatting away and ready to sit in front of the fire. He lived for about another year.

The experience with Gale has now stood Gina well. She lives on a farm where there are lakes. There has been a number of occasions where a swan has needed rescuing. Where most people would not know what to do Gina has no qualms in jumping into the lakes and wading in to grab a swan. There is no fear at all and she has also managed to rescue many birds and wildlife.

This book came about for a similar reason, animal rescue. In the middle of the night, I was woken by one of my cats unmistakable call that she had bought me a gift, a mouse. I rescued the mouse, then lost my balance and to save myself falling to the ground slammed my hand so hard on the worktop in the utility room I broke my little finger. A visit to A&E and a splint was put on, which meant I could not write or sew and I am never happier than when I have a needle in my hands. I was stumped, with six weeks of having to wear this splint, not good. Then it was found that I could indeed type after a fashion, using Gina's iPad, Hooray!!! The notes of all those years ago were brought out of cold storage and this is the result which I hope will give you some pleasure.

Thank you for reading.

Acknowledgments

To my son Alex for bringing Gale home. For giving her the opportunity to have a life and for all of us the experience of having her as part of our family.

To Brian for working out how to feed Gale.

To Gina for helping bring this together.

To all my neighbours who were always a support in my work with the animals, especially Joy and her daughter Samantha.

Bill Pethrington, my vet at the time who helped with so many in need.

To the local journalists and TV station for the work they did in reporting on Gale's life with us: *Western Gazette* and *Western Daily Press*.

Sir Peter Scott.

To the Tesco stores and other shops in Yeovil for allowing Gale in their shops.

To Sutton Bingham Reservoir for giving me permission to teach Gale to fly using their lake.

The British Museum.

The Local Police.

To the Late Lord Bath: Henry Frederick Thynne, Sixth Marquess of Bath for his help in giving Gale and Sydney a home.

To all those that were part of this incredible journey that I have not mentioned.

www.ingramcontent.com/pod-product-compliance
Ingram Content Group UK Ltd.
Pitfield, Milton Keynes, MK11 3LW, UK
UKHW022225270825
462282UK00002B/3